MAKING A PEDIGREE

MAKING
A
PEDIGREE

John Unett

Second Edition
with new Preface and Bibliography

GENEALOGICAL PUBLISHING CO., INC.
Baltimore   1971

First published in London 1961
Second edition 1971 published in the
United States of America by
GENEALOGICAL PUBLISHING CO., INC.
Baltimore, Maryland
in conjunction with
David & Charles (Publishers) Limited
Newton Abbot Devon England

Library of Congress Catalog Card Number 75-141813
International Standard Book Number 0-8063-0464-2

Printed in Great Britain
by Redwood Press Limited Trowbridge Wilts
for David & Charles (Publishers) Limited
Newton Abbot Devon

PREFACE

I HAVE found it necessary to make only a few changes to the text of the first edition, yet great changes have taken place in the genealogical world since I first wrote this introduction to the subject of family history.

As the population of England becomes increasingly mobile, and the growth of vast housing estates emphasises how alike we are all becoming, so the desire is growing to break away, to find a separate identity, to go back to the source of the family, to find where the family character through past generations was moulded in the hope that in some degree stability and continuity may restore our individuality.

When I first joined the Society of Genealogists in 1933, the membership remained static; new members balanced those dying, the Society just kept afloat. All that has now changed. New members pour in. Interest in genealogy is enormous, and growing.

This is the individual in action, proving that he is more than just a statistic. If this little book does anything to help that movement forward, I shall be very happy.

Malvern 1970

John Unett

INTRODUCTION

W I T H the increasing interest in genealogy, there is a need for a short book to guide the searcher into the easiest and best way to work. As he will, in the course of his searches, be led from one class of documents to another, this book is intended to indicate only the main sources from which the world of genealogy opens out. It is not suggested, for example, that he should search the documents in the order in which they are here considered for he may find it more convenient to be led by the results he obtains. But it sometimes happens that a new source is required, or a source is found which the searcher does not understand. This book is intended to suggest new sources, and to outline how they came into existence and what kind of material they contain.

A specimen pedigree is given of an imaginary family of MARSH, the figures by each entry relating to separate sheets on which details of each member of the family are entered. Sheet 27, for example, contains details of CHARLES BAILEY MARSH entered, not chronologically, but as the genealogist came across them—

SHEET 27

CHARLES BAILEY MARSH   =1. PENELOPE STONE
of Broadwood Hall,   m. about 1800
Clungunford, co. Salop.
His w. proved 19.7.1831
by Rebecca (Tebbs 429 PCC)
but adm. granted to John
Watts 9.4.1847 *de bonis non.*   =2. REBECCA She
Charles B. left *all* property   afterwards m. John
to Rebecca. Univ. Coll.   Watts to whom
Oxford 13.11.1795 aged 17,   Broadwood Hall des-
therefore b. 1778. (Hopton   cended. Rebecca d.
814) Died on Thursday 12 May 1831   19.4.1846 intestate.
aged 53 at Broadwood Hall   Buried at Clungunford
(Salopian Journal 18 May 1831)
Inherited silver from mother and
proved her will on 17.9.1811.
Inherited £200 from his uncle
Thomas

By this means the main pedigree is kept free of detail and a clear picture obtained of the relationship between different generations. This is particularly useful when the search covers a long period and where several members of the family bear the same Christian name.

Throughout this book the following abbreviations will be used. These are the accepted ones, the apparent confusion between English and Latin being unavoidable—

b.	—	born
bap.	—	baptised
m.	—	married
d.	—	died
bur.	—	buried
s.	—	son (or, sometimes, succeeded)
dau.	—	daughter
s. & h.	—	son and heir
s.p.	—	sine prole
d.s.p.	—	died sine prole
d.s.p.m.	—	died sine prole mascula
dum	—	died unmarried (sometimes d. unm.)
c.	—	circa

Wherever possible, locations of records are given, but this can only be done in the case of national collections such as the series of Rolls at the Public Record Office. Many of the genealogist's facts will come from local records, in the custody of county librarians, parish priests, and private libraries. For these the searcher must make his own inquiries for they are being continually added to as the work of collecting and indexing progresses.

The method of introduction to each class of records is by examples so that the searcher can tell at a glance whether the source is likely to give him the kind of information he needs. Experienced searchers will, it is hoped, forgive the analyses that follow some of the examples; they are given in the hope of helping someone new to genealogy to extract the maximum information from each document and to show how apparently unimportant facts may lead the searcher to another and richer source.

FAMILY OF MARSH

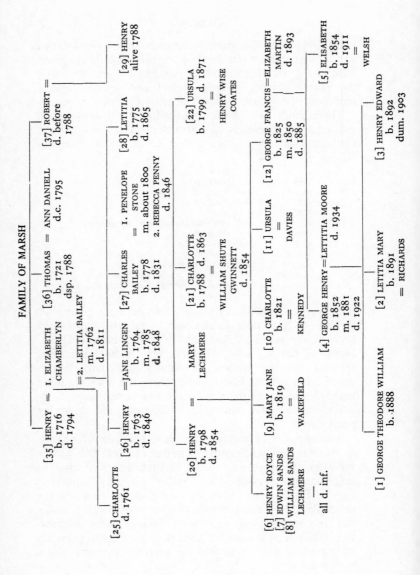

CONTENTS

Chapter 1

PARISH REGISTERS AND THE PARISH CHEST

T H E genealogist's first source is, of course, the living family, verbal information probably carrying him back a hundred years, and at least giving him the places where his family lived. This brings him in touch with parish registers and other records in the custody of incumbents. They will therefore be the next source of his research.

Parish Registers were first begun under an order by Thomas Cromwell, Vicar-General in 1538 requiring a record to be kept by the incumbent of christenings, marriages and burials. Entries were to be made in the presence of the churchwardens and the book kept locked in the chest. Later, in 1597 and 1603, orders were issued that copies of the entries were to be sent to the Bishops' Registries, and genealogists can sometimes fill in gaps in the original registers from these transcripts.

In practice, though the orders were clear, few registers are to be found earlier than about 1580. Often there are isolated entries in the first volume showing that an attempt was made to comply with the orders, but regular entries on which a genealogist can rely do not appear before about 1600. Not only were incumbents lax in carrying out the orders, but there was great destruction during the Civil War when documents of all kinds suffered. If, therefore, the searcher finds a register for the early period he should remember that there may have been many christenings, marriages and burials omitted and that the children registered as christened are not necessarily the only issue of a particular marriage. Moreover, infant mortality was exceptionally heavy until recent times, and many children recorded as christened may not, in fact, have reached maturity.

There were many attempts to make these registers reliable and comprehensive. An order in 1681 compelled parents to register every birth; but as there was a fee of 6d., this Act was widely ignored. Later, further charges were levied on births, marriages and burials as a form of taxation, and this further encouraged poor people to evade registration.

For about the last hundred years, entries in registers can be taken as reliable, but before that their reliability decreases as the searcher goes back. Yet what is unreliable is not the entries themselves, but omissions. If an entry is recorded, there is seldom reason to suppose that it is not accurate: what is dangerous is to assume that the pedigree can be based on those entries as recording all the births, marriages and deaths that took place in that parish. One may find, from a will perhaps, that a member of the family died in a certain year and that he lived in a certain parish. The fact of there being no record in the register does not mean that he was not buried there. Registers, in other words, are reliable as to the entries they contain, but are by no means comprehensive.

Most parish registers are in the custody of the incumbent, kept either in his personal possession, or in the church. There is, however, a growing practice of depositing all but the current register at the local library, often in the county town. A few counties have Parish Register Societies which print these registers, and the genealogist may find that his parish is one that has been done. If the volume has an index, his search may be only a matter of moments, and he can extract all the entries of his family over all the years. But these societies are usually hampered by lack of funds, and, with rising printing costs, even fewer are appearing than before.

Where the register is not at the local library, and if a visit to the parish is impossible owing to distance, or pressure of other work, the entries can be obtained from the rector. But too often correspondents imagine that this is a service to which they are entitled; they expect him to spend hours searching his registers; so the searcher should make it clear that he is prepared to pay.

Monumental Inscriptions are rarely listed in registers,

though occasionally they form part of a parish history. More often, the searcher has no alternative but to go to the church. They are probably the most reliable of all sources of information. Sometimes they give the house in which the deceased lived, the names of his parents; they will almost certainly give the date of death and age, thereby giving the year of birth. If he was someone of importance, there may be a coat of arms, and this should be copied with particular care about differences or quarterings.

Regarding the rector's other documents, a search there also takes time. He may have poor-law records, minutes of parish meetings, records of enclosures, a history of road repairs before they were taken over by the counties—many records may lie in his church chest, and the best person to carry out the search is the genealogist himself for he knows what material suits his purpose. This book is intended for the genealogist who wants to do as much as he can in order to avoid expense, reserving such money as he has for the early centuries where documents can only be read by experts. Parish registers, and the other documents in the custody of incumbents, should all be within the capacity of the genealogist who has a little latin and a little experience of early writing.

As an example of the records that may be available in a parish, here is a list of those for the parish of Headcorn in Kent as listed in the Guide to the Kent County Archives Office—

Churchwardens' rates and accounts, 1638-1836. Vestry minute book, 1805-40. Overseers' rates and accounts, 1689-1841, including lists of paupers giving ages and disabilities, 1689-1707; relief books, 1807-36; clothing books, 1783-1829; parish bills, 1815-42; settlement papers, 1663-1851; apprenticeship papers, 1639-1777; bastardy papers, 1727-1833; work books of paupers hired, 1819-35; emigration papers, including list giving names and ages of families wishing to emigrate to Canada, 1829-43. Valuation lists and income tax assessments, c. 1837-94. Deposited railway plans, 1883-1926. Surveyors' rates, 1664-1841; accounts, 1815-41. Charity papers, 1596-1793. Tithe map,

1843; altered apportionments, etc., 1839-1936.

Few parishes have such a wealth of records, but there is such a variety of subjects that no genealogist interested in the parish can afford to pass by such sources. They take him right into the parish, among the yeomen and husbandmen as few other records can.

Chapter 2

WILLS AND ADMINISTRATIONS

U N T I L recent times, land was not disposed of by will but by the normal process of settlement, whether the land was free-hold or copyhold. Early wills, therefore, deal exclusively with personalty—livestock, household goods, family possessions, money, and such specific items as the testator wished to descend to particular members of the family. In more recent years, with the end of copyhold tenure, wills give more in-formation about a testator's estate, and from them the genealogist, in the early stages of building up his pedigree, can obtain valuable information not only of the testator's descendents, but of his standing in the community.

When the searcher reaches the eighteenth century, though he loses details of land, he sometimes finds inventories, and these give even more personal details than later wills: often the contents of each room of the house, details of farm stock, how many sheep and cattle, the quantity of growing crops, details of debts, all of great importance to the writer of a family history, and much of it valuable for his pedigree. The inventory often shows something of inter-family finance, loans made by one brother to another, information not dis-closed by the will alone.

At the present time, the facilities for genealogists are un-satisfactory as far as searching wills is concerned. In order to explain how the present position has arisen a few words may be helpful about the procedure for registering wills. Often, when it was clear that no dispute would arise, they were never proved, and some cases where a testator is known to have made a will but it cannot be found may be thus accounted for. On the other hand, where there might be dispute over it, the will might be proved in the most superior court possible to give it authority. There was not one recognized way of dealing with wills.

Power to grant probate was vested in all manner of courts, from the small local manor court to the great archiepiscopal courts of Canterbury and York. A small man, having no property outside his own manor, would probably have his will proved in the manor court, if it had that power. Generally speaking, except for important or disputatious wills, the executor, or executrix, would prove in the lowest court partly for convenience and also on account of cost. Where a testator held property in more than one manor, or ecclesiastical district, his will would normally be proved in the more senior court. If his property was widely spread, it would be proved either in the Prerogative Court of York, or Canterbury, the latter being the senior court in England.

For centuries, therefore, hundreds of courts all over England were proving wills, some just bundling them up as they came in until they were destroyed to make more room, others being registered in Act Books, others copied out in extenso in registers. In more recent times they began to be collected into centres, usually the episcopal centre, where they were held, often without an index or any suggestion of what period they covered, or what parishes or manors. Then they were again moved, the Hereford wills for example went to Llandaff, then more recently to the National Library of Wales. In Birmingham, for many years, were, among others, wills proved in the Lichfield courts. My latest information is that they are now back at Lichfield. There seems to be no one to make a plan.

The genealogist probably goes first to Somerset House to inspect the wills proved within the last hundred years, then down to where the PCC transcripts are kept. From these two sources he will be able to fill in at least the last hundred years of his pedigree, and from the PCC wills to collect many others of his family which he will at that stage be unable to fit into his pedigree.

The service offered by these depositories varies greatly. Some have no freelance archivists, the genealogist having to make his own arrangements by employing someone outside.

The Society of Genealogists, in its quarterly periodical, gives lists of searchers in all parts of the country. Some depositories have photocopying machines and the searcher is thereby able to obtain copies of original documents often much cheaper than even an extract would cost. These machines have now been widely installed and are of great assistance. Yet there is no standard on which he can rely in every case: some depositories are efficient and helpful, answering letters promptly and carrying out work quickly. At Aberystwyth, for example, inaccessible to most searchers, the National Library of Wales has not only an up-to-date photocopying machine, but an efficient and helpful way of dealing with customers. Preliminary searches are made without charge, subsequent work is done promptly, and invoicing is done in a businesslike manner.

When he has completed his work at Somerset House, and used such distant services as he needs, he visits the archivist at the nearest town to inquire about local wills. He may find the indexes scanty, perhaps manuscript books, or he may be told that the wills are still kept in their original bundles either alphabetically, or under the original courts in which they were proved. There may be bundles of wills never indexed, he may be told that there are also bundles of administrations not yet listed. It is true that a will is of interest to few people, limited to members of the same family, local historians, and perhaps to someone writing a history of a particular trade in which that person was engaged. When, therefore, the county archivist, or librarian, or whoever is in control, plans how best to use his limited funds, he naturally chooses first the classes of records of most general interest. Wills come low down on that list.

Here is a late eighteenth century will, of Thomas Marsh, shown in the pedigree as b. 1721: d.s.p. 1788. The original will, of which a photocopy was obtained, is at Aberystwyth. I have chosen this as an example of how one can arrive at a decision that there were no issue of a marriage, and how the maximum information can be drawn from a will, also how further probable deductions are, because they are not certain, omitted from the pedigree until later confirmed from some other source.

'THOMAS MARSH of Sutton St. Michael in the County of Here-for Being of Sound Mind, Memory and understanding Do make & Ordain Publish and Declare This my Last Will and Testament in Manner and form following (That is to Say) First it is My Will, and Desire, That all my Just Debts, (and Funeral Expenses not Exceeding Ten Pounds) Shall be fully Paid and Satisfied, By my Executor herein After Named as also The Charge of Proving This my Will.

Imprimis) I give to my Dear and Loving Wife Ann The Interest yearly Arising From Fourteen Hundred Pounds During her Natural Life, and all Interest That shall or may be Due Unto me on The Securities at The time of my Decease and her Recept, Shall Be Their Sufficient Discharge for The Interest Then Due, and The Interest yearly Arising also—and also The Use of all my Household Goods of Whatsoever Kind or Nature During her Natural Life and after my Wife's Decease it is my Will and Desire That The affore Mentioned Sum of Fourteen Hundred Pounds, Be Disposed off, With all my Household Goods By my Executor in Manner following That is to Say) I also Give to my Niece Letitia Marsh Two Hundred Pounds, I also Give to my Nephew, Charles Bayley Marsh Two Hundred Pounds, which money Being Left me By my Father— and They Being Children of my Elder Brother, I also Give to My Nephew Thomas Marsh, Three Hundred and fifty Pounds, and all my Household Goods, after my Wifes Decease, I also give to My Niece Sarah Turner, The Interest Arising From Three Hundred Pounds, to Be Paid Unto her yearly During her Natural Life, and her Recept to Be my Executors Sufficient Discharge For the Same, and at her Decease The Principal Stock off The afforesaid Three Hundred Pounds to Be equally Divided Between her Children, NB: Which Legacies are not to Be Paid, till The Expiration of Six Months after The Decease of my Dear and Loving Wife Ann, and in Case Either of my Nephews or Nieces Should Die affore Their Legacies Become Payable Then That Legacie or Legacies to Be Equally Divided

Between The Surviving one, Named in my Will—and Lastly I also Make Constitute and appoint my Nephew Henry Marsh, Son of my Late Brother Robert Marsh Sole Executor, To Whom I Give out of My Personal Estate The Sum of Three Hundred and Sixty Pounds—In Wittness Whereof, I The Said Thomas Marsh, have to This my Last Will and Testament Set my hand and Seal This Twelfth Day of September in The year of Our Lord God one Thousand Seven Hundred and Eighty Six

Signed Sealed Published and Declared By The Said Thomas Marsh, The Testator as his Last Will and testament In The Presence of Us Who at his Desire and Request and in his Sight and Presence Subscribed Our Names as Witness Thereto
      Witness to The Execution of
      This Will . . .
          Ws: Allen, Jnr
          Edmund Barry   *Thomas Marsh*
          Thomas Williams

(My first Codicil) It is my will and desire that my Dear and Loving Wife Ann should have yearly paid her, the Interest of Fifty five Pounds During her Natural Life; over and above what is expressed in my Will; and at her Decease it is my further Will and Desire that Henry Marsh Son of my Late Brother Robert Marsh should have the afore mentioned Sum of fifty five Pounds in Witness whereof I have hereunto Set my hand and Seal this fifth Day of January one Thousand seven hundred and Eighty eight.
          Witness   *Thomas Marsh*
      Elizabeth Turner
      E. Thomas
      John Constable

                                    31 May 1788
      Henry Marsh the Executor in this Will named was then Sworn in due form of Law to this Will and Codicile Before Me

                          R. Underwood
                              Surrogate

This Will with a Codicil annexed was proved at Hereford 14th June 1788 before the Worl. George Harris, D.D., Vic. Genl. & by the Oath of Henry Marsh the sole Executor within named To whom etc./.'

The following facts can be drawn from this will, those considered definite appearing in the pedigree referred to earlier—

1. Thomas Marsh was of the parish of Sutton St Michael, and died between 5 January 1788 (when he signed the codicil) and 31 May 1788 (when his will was proved).

2. His wife Ann was alive on 5 January 1788 (when codicil signed) but not necessarily on 31 May when the will was proved.

3. No mention of where he is to be buried.

4. No mention of children. All his property, including household goods, left to nephews and nieces.

5. Nephew Henry, son of late brother Robert, appointed executor. When considered with above disposal of personalty, strong indication either that no issue of marriage, or else that they were all dead by 12 September 1786 (when will signed).

6. Niece Letitia (daughter of elder brother) alive 12.9.1786.

7. Nephew Charles Bayley (son of elder brother) alive 12.9.1786. As they are dealt with jointly, they are presumably both children of the same brother.

8. Nephew Thomas, presumably not another brother of Letitia and Charles Bayley for he is dealt with separately, alive 12.9.1786. He inherits all household goods after wife's decease.

9. Niece Sarah Turner alive and presumably married by 12.9.1786 (no indication of whose daughter she is).

The following small pedigree can now be built up from this single will, and, presuming for the moment that no other facts are available from any other source, such information as 'died before . . .' or 'alive on . . .' is used until more precise information is available.

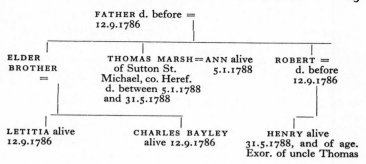

The name of the 'elder brother' is not given, but the indication is that he was still alive at 12.9.1786, for when the testator speaks of Henry he describes him as son of 'my Late Brother Robert', which is not how he describes the children of the elder brother. The position of his nephew Thomas is impossible to determine for there is no indication of whose son he is. This is unfortunate because he bears the same name as the testator and is his residuary legatee, but it would be wrong to guess that he was a son of either the elder brother, or of Robert. His position in the pedigree must be left until later.

Other points worth mentioning are that Ann is shown in the pedigree as alive on the date the codicil was signed, but not when the will was proved. She may have been alive then (she was, as it happens, for her will has been found and is given below, but from her husband's will all we can be sure of is that she was alive when he signed it). As regards his father, all we know is that he was dead by 12.9.1786. He may have died many years before, but we do not know, any more than we know his name. Again, this information has been obtained from other sources, but from the will of Thomas Marsh all we can enter is what is shown. Similarly with the testator's brother Robert. We do not know when he died, nor when his son Henry was born, all we know is that Henry was of sufficient age to prove the will in 1788, and that his father died before 12.9.1786.

Nothing can be done about his niece Sarah Turner; there is nothing to show where she fits in the pedigree. Like the nephew Thomas, she must be left in abeyance until from some other source we find whose daughter she is. Another source of error is to assume that because a will says that a legacy shall be paid after the death of Sarah Turner equally to her children that at the time of the will she was married and had children. The legacy may have been made even before she married; Turner may be her maiden name for all the will tells us. Only when children are named, or in some other way identified (as, for example, 'to each of the four children of my niece . . .'), can they be assumed to have been born.

Signatures on wills are one of the most valuable sources of information. Comparatively few people could write, or even sign their names, and the ability to do so is some evidence of education. But more than that, they are useful for identification. In times when it was not customary to give more than one Christian name, often members of the family bore the same name and it is not always easy to distinguish between them. If the signature appears on the will, however, that particular person can be identified, and if other documents appear, leases for example, or witnesses to other wills, that signature overcomes such difficulty.

The will of Ann Marsh, wife of Thomas Marsh, has also survived, and is given below. When the wife predeceased the husband there was often no will, and only too often in cases where she survived him she is ultimately found to have died intestate, as we saw with Rebecca, wife of Charles Bayley Marsh. Wills of female members of the family, as already indicated, can be the greatest value to the genealogist : they sometimes mention many relatives, leaving them little things, pieces of jewellery, or household articles. Men, on the other hand, usually deal in broad terms with their possessions. Ann Marsh's will, for example, is full of information; precise, detailed, unambiguous.

"I ANN MARSH of Sutton St. Michael in the County of Hereford being of sound mind and memory, and understanding Do make ordain Publish and declare this my last Will and Testament in manner and form following (that is to say) First it is my Will and desire that all my Just Debts and Funeral Expenses shall be paid and discharged by my Executor herein after named As also the Charge of Proving this my Will N.B. which said Debts and Expenses and the Charge of Proving of this my Will is to be paid out of my Personal Estate or Money and Interest of Money that shall or will be due to me at my Decease IMPRIMIS I give and bequeath to my Niece Shusannah Danniel (Daughter of my Brother William Danniel) all my Linen and Clothes and all the Household Goods and Furniture that I have bought and paid for since the Death of my Late Husband. ITEM, I give and bequeath to my Brother William Danniel the Sum of five Pounds. I also give and bequeath to my Nephew William Jones (Son of my Late Sister Sarah Jones) the Sum of Ten Pounds. And all the Rest, Residue or Remainder of Money and Interest of Money that shall or will be due to me at my Decease I give and bequeath to my Brother William Danniel's Children to be equally divided between them. And Lastly I also make Constitute and appoint Henry Marsh (that is Executor to my Late Husband's Will) Sole Executor to this my last Will and Testament In witness whereof I the said Ann Marsh have to this my last Will and Testament set my hand and Seal this ninth day of April in the Year of our Lord one thousand seven hundred and ninety five.

The mark of Ann Marsh

X

Signed, Sealed, Published and declared by the said Ann Marsh the Testatrix as and for her last Will and Testament in the presence of us who at her desire and Request and in her sight and presence Subscribed our Names as Witnesses thereto

Major Baker

John Constable

William Constable

21st October 1797 Sole Executor sworn. Proved at Hereford 22nd November 1797.'

Following on the practice already suggested of building up a pedigree from the will we now have—

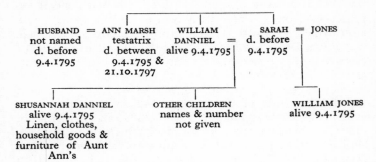

HUSBAND	=	ANN MARSH	WILLIAM		SARAH	=	JONES
not named		testatrix	DANNIEL	=	d. before		
d. before		d. between	alive 9.4.1795		9.4.1795		
9.4.1795		9.4.1795 &					
		21.10.1797					

SHUSANNAH DANNIEL	OTHER CHILDREN	WILLIAM JONES
alive 9.4.1795	names & number	alive 9.4.1795
Linen, clothes,	not given	
household goods &		
furniture of Aunt		
Ann's		

It is possible, of course, to make these entries direct on to the husband's pedigree. But the advantage of making a separate pedigree for each will, limited strictly to the facts in that will, is that they can always be checked later and are not confused by facts from another source which may not be mentioned. In the above, for example, is 'Husband, not named d. before 9.4.1795' because that is all the information given by the will. The fact that his name was Thomas, and that he died between 5.1.1788 and 31.5.1788 comes from another source. Similarly, on the pedigree made from the husband's will, it was impossible to add the date of Ann's death, or the period during which she must have died, for the same reason. These additional facts come together on the individual's sheet, and on the main pedigree.

The fact of Ann not signing her name is of no significance: it was common among women well into the nineteenth century, even members of the yeoman and middle classes.

From these two wills it seems almost certain that both Thomas and Ann d.s.p. Thomas left the residue of his estate to his wife for life, then to nephews and nieces: Ann likewise. In neither will is there any indication of children. Further evidence will have to be sought from the parish registers of Sutton St Michael, and, if the marriage is not there, further searches should be made in adjoining parishes to see if any christenings followed the marriage. But the indications are that there were no issue.

Now, it so happens that there is a tablet on the wall of Sutton St Michael church bearing these words—

> Underneath lyeth the remains of Thomas Marsh He departed this life 17 March 1788 aged 67 years

So we make two additions to his sheet, and two further entries on the main pedigree—the actual date of death, 17 March 1788 instead of the entry 'between 5.1.1788 and 31.5.1788', and at least the year of birth even if the date and month are not yet known, i.e. 1721.

Chapter 3

STYLE OF WILLS OVER THE CENTURIES

F o R the strict genealogist, a change in the form of a will is of no importance, but for the historian it is part of the changing pattern. Everything will be brought into his history if he is to give a true representation of his family's life, economic history for example, national events which affected their way of living, but also these little reflections of mood and emotion picked up from such documents as wills.

It is true, of course, that the wording was largely in the hands of lawyers, but there is no reason to suppose that a lawyer chose the form that he himself preferred rather than one to suit his client. The language of each century represents its time.

Here is the will of a prosperous farmer a hundred years earlier than those previously given—

'IN THE NAME OF GOD AMEN! the 14th day of Aprill 1691 I George Norton of Whitbourne in the County of Buckingham Yeoman for good causes me thereunto moveing, but being in perfect mind and memory (Blessed be God) and calling to mind my mortality, believing it is appointed for all men once to die; do make and ordaine my last Will and Testament in manner and forme following. First I give my Soul into the hands of my most merciful God most humbly beseeching his acceptance of it and for my Body I commend it to the earth to be decently buried in Xtian buriall nothing doubting by the omnipotent power of my Saviour Jesus Xt both God and man of a glorious resurrection. For my worldly Estate that God hath blessed me with I give devise bequeath and dispose the same in manner and forme following . . .'

Here we have another of about the same date of an esquire living in the same parish—

'IN THE NAME OF GOD AMEN the thirtyeth day of Aprill in the yeare of our Lord God one Thousand six hundred and seaventie two I Francis Walsham of Whitbourne in the County of Buckingham Esquire doe make and ordaine this my last Will and Testament in manner and forme followinge That is to say First I humbly recommend my soule unto Almighty God my Maker And to Jesus Christ my deare and Blessed Saviour through whose onely merritts I hope for a joyfull resurrection unto eternall life, And my body to the Earth to be buried in decent manner att the discretion of my Executrix hereafter named AND as touchinge my worldly Estate Goods and Chattells wherewith it hath pleased God to blesse mee I doe by this my last Will devise and despose as followeth . . .'

The same feeling is reflected in each. There were, of course, important distinctions between an esquire and a yeoman, but then, as today, the classes overlapped. If we could have had each one's personal expression of his feelings we would then be closer to such distinctions as existed; as it is, we must be content with the intervention of the lawyer to some extent standardizing the expression. But the feeling is there, the scent of the century.

Next, a lady from the same part of the country, a more flowery opening, perhaps reflecting the Restoration—

'IN THE NAME OF GOD AMEN The tenth day of December in the fifteenth yeare of the Raign of our Sovereign Lord Charles the Second by the grace of God King of England Scotland France & Ireland Defender of the faith etc AND in the yeare of our Lord one Thousand six hundred Sixty Three; I Elizabeth Hatford of the parrish of Putley in the County of Buckingham widdowe being weake in body but of a good and pfect memory Doe make Publish and Declare this my last Will & Testament in writing in manner and forme following; First I give and bequeathe my Soule to Allmighty Good my Creator;

assuredly hoping in & through the merrits Death and passion
of Jesus Christ my Saviour that the same shall bee made
ptaker of the Joyes of life everlasting; and my Corps Committ
to Christian buriall according to the discretion of my
Executrix hereafter named And as touching my Worldly good
estate wherewith God hath enriched mee I devise give and
bequeath thereof as hereinafter followeth . . .'

The disposal of her goods and the appointment of her
brother-in-law as overseer do not take more than a few lines,
considerably shorter than the opening. This particular will
was signed and witnessed, but there was no issue of probate
so it may be a case of a simple will (she left everything to her
daughter) not being proved.

Going back a hundred years, is a will of 1548, dated, as was
often the custom, by the regnal year instead of the Christian
calendar. There is nothing to show the status of the testator,
but from other sources he is known to have been of good
yeoman stock—

'IN THE NAME OF GOD AMEN I Richard Barrett off Cradley bying
sycke in bodye but in pfett mayie make testment the fyrst
day off July in second yer off ye rayn off Our Sovereign Lord
Edward the syxt by the grace off God off England France &
Ireland King Defender off ye fryth and in earth the (illegible)
        off the   off England & Ireland Fyrst I commend
my soule to almighty God desyryng off his mercy to pardon
it when his pleasing is also I bequethe to John my son my
            and I bequeath the rest of my goodes to my wyfe
whom I make my sole executrix wytnessed Johon & Wyllm.'

There was little organized spelling until the eighteenth
century, it not being uncommon to find a man spelling his own
name in different ways in the same document. The above will,
damaged on one side, was neither signed, witnessed, nor
proved. But such information as there is can be extracted.
How such a document reaches a depository cannot be known.
It may be a copy of one originally proved in a manor court,

the copy surviving the original. Nevertheless, it is possible to build up a small pedigree establishing a few facts which may later fit into the pedigree.

```
RICHARD BARRETT    =   wife, alive 1.7.1548
   of Cradley, will          |
   dated 1.7.1548,           |
    sick in body             |
                             |
        JOHN BARRETT
        alive 1.7.1548
```

Later it may be possible to find more about him from, for example, manor rolls if they can be found. His father's will has also been found, so something more is known already of the family. It is most unlikely that his burial will appear in the parish register, for they had only been instituted a few years and few country parishes have them as early as this. Pedigrees become progressively more difficult to compile as we go back, here we have one example of why. Yet even so little information is better than none. We know that this Richard was living 'sycke in bodye' at that place in 1548, and that he had a son John living, and a wife, both near enough to witness his will. The blanks in the will must unfortunately be left, even though it is sometimes possible to guess what has been lost. But it should be possible at any time to take an item in the pedigree and go to its source, whether it be a will, a parish register, Chancery Proceeding, manor roll, or any other document and find that indisputable fact recorded.

Back another hundred years, we find the same basic form though in this instance in latin, here translated—

'IN THE NAME OF GOD AMEN. I John Evot formerly citizen and draper of London, being of sound mind and good memory on 12th November 1435 and the fourteenth year of king Henry the sixth after the conquest, compose make and ordain this my present will in the manner which follows:
In the first place I bequeath and commend my soul to God the omnipotent creator and my saviour and to the blessed virgin Mary his mother and to all the saints, and my body to

be buried in the cemetery of St. Paul's church, London, called 'Pardon chirchawe' if I happen to die in London, otherwise wherever God shall dispose or ordain . . .'

He then bequeaths several legacies to the church at Yalding (Kent) and to St Gregory next to St Paul's, and to his executor and others. Then—

'The residue of all my goods and chattels and dues wherever they exist, after the due payment of my burial duly and honestly made and the completion of this my present will, I give and bequeath wholly to my executors to do, dispose of and distribute for my soul and the souls of my parents and friends and of all to whom I am obliged and for all the faithful departed, so that by celebrating masses, distributing to the poor, and by other pious uses and works of charity they shall think and hope to please God and to profit the safety of my soul and the other aforesaid souls.'

He then refers to certain lands and tenements in co. Kent which he purchased as in fee simple and of which divers persons were enfeoffed by him in trust to his use and directs—

'. . . my executors shall sell all the lands and tenements as quickly as they are well able to do after my death in the best way they are able and know how, without deceipt or fraud, willing that my feofees shall make an estate to him or those to whom the said sale shall be made when they shall be duly required by my said executors, and that the money produced and received from the same sale shall be disposed of by my executors in buying ornaments for the said church of Yalding greatly necessary to it, according to the good discretion of my executors, to remain there, so that my soul shall have the greater special recommendation by the prayers of the parishioners and in other divine services.'

The will was proved on 28 February 1435/6 in the Prerogative Court of Canterbury by the executor. This type of will does not help the genealogist as he says nothing about his family, but it gives us a picture of the man, and of the state of England at the time.

Chapter 4

ADMINISTRATIONS AND INVENTORIES

ADMINISTRATIONS, where the deceased fails to leave a will, or where executors die or refuse to act, are usually disappointing for the genealogist. Application is made, usually by a near relative, and the grant made to him, or her, to administer the estate either in accordance with the terms of the will, if there is one, or under the laws of intestacy.

In the case of Charles Bailey Marsh, a grant was made to John Watts on 9.4.1847 to administer the goods left unadministered by his wife. He was no doubt chosen because all Charles Bailey's property descended to his widow, who later married John Watts, so he would be the best person to continue the administration, although, in that case, there were closer relatives of Charles Bailey Marsh available.

Here is the standard form of administration, sometimes the top portion is in latin and the lower in English—

KNOW all men by these presents that We George Edwards of the parish of Bitterley in the county of Salop, Mason, Richard Millechamp of the parish of Bitterley aforesaid in the same county Husbandman and John Knowles of the City of Hereford yeoman are held and firmly bound unto the Right Revd. Father in God James by divine permission Lord Bishop of Hereford in the sum of Five Hundred pounds of good and lawful money of Great Britain to be paid unto the said Right Reverend Father or to his certain Attorney his executors Administrators or Assigns To which Payment well and truly to be made We oblige ourselves and each and every of us by himself jointly & severally for the whole our and each and every of our Heirs Executors and Administrators firmly by these Presents sealed with our seals dated the Eighteenth

day of March in the Fifteenth Year of the Reign of our
Sovereign Lord George the Third by the Grace of God of Great
Britain, France and Ireland King Defender of the Faith and so
forth And in the Year of our Lord one Thousand Seven hundred
and seventy five.

The Condition of this obligation is such that if the above
bounden George Edwards the natural & lawful son and Ad-
ministrator of all the goods Chattels and Credits of William
Edwards late of the parish of Bitterley, widower, deceased do
make or cause to be made a true and perfect Inventory of all
and singular the Goods Chattels and Credits of the said
deceased which have or shall come to the hands, possession
or Knowledge of him the said George Edwards or into the
hands and possession of any person or persons for him and the
same so made do exhibit or cause to be exhibited into the
Registry of the Consistory Court of the Diocese of Hereford
at or before the last day of April next ensuing and the same
Goods, Chattels and Credits and all other the Goods, Chattels
and Credits of the said deceased at the time of his death which
at any time after shall come to the hands or possession of the
said George Edwards or into the hands and possession of any
other Person or Persons for him to well and truly administer
according to Law And further do make or cause to be made a
true and just Accompt of his said Administration at or before
the last day of March 1776 and all the Rest and Residue of the
said Goods, Chattels and Credits which shall be found remaining upon the said Administrators Accompt the same
being first examined and allowed of by the judge or judges
for the time being of the said Court shall deliver and pay unto
such Person or Persons respectively as the said Judge or Judges
by his or their Decree or Sentence pursuant to the true intent
and Meaning of a late Act of Parliament made in the two and
twentieth and three and twentieth Years of the Reign of our
late Sovereign Lord King Charles the Second entitled an Act
for the better settling of Intestates' Estates shall limit and
appoint And if it shall hereafter appear that any last Will and
Testament was made by the said Deceased and the Executor

or Executors therein named do exhibit the same into the said
Court making Request to have it allowed and approved accord-
ingly if the said George Edwards above bounden being thereunto required do render and deliver the said Letters of Administration (Approbation of such Testament being first had
and made) in the said Court then this Obligation to be Void,
or else to remain in full force and Virtue.

Sealed and delivered in the presence of—	*The mark of George Edwards*
	X
Geo Holland	*Richard Millechamp* *John Knowles*

18 Day of March Then appeared personally George Edwards
and alledged that William Edwards late of the parish of
Bitterley in the County of Salop and Diocese of Hereford
widower deceased lately died Intestate or without making any
last Will or Testament That he is the natural & lawful son
and one of the next of kin of the said deceased Wherefore he
prayed that letters of Action of the Goods Chattels and Credits
of the said deceased might be granted to him under proper
Security

> We grant Letters of Administration
> according to the above petition the
> said George Edwards being first Sworn
> in due form of Law
> > Before me
> > *W Skinner, Surrogate*

Even from this meagre document some genealogical information can be obtained—

WILLIAM EDWARDS d. before 18.3.1775	=	Wife, predeceased husband

GEORGE EDWARDS
alive 18.3.1775,
mason of Bitterley.
co. Salop. Took out
L. of A. for father

When later sources are inspected this information may be useful. George, for example, is known not only to be alive on 18.3.1775, but of sufficient age to take out letters of administration, certainly not a child. If, for example, we found in the parish registers a George Edwards baptized in, say, 1770 we would know that it could not be the same. If, to take another example, we found in the register dated 1770 the burial of a George Edwards we would know that it could not be the son of William, any more than could a burial of a George Edwards in, say, 1855, for he would then be about 100 years old—possible, but too improbable to be accepted without other evidence.

I have not been able to find the Inventory corresponding to that administration, so must turn to another. The information is not always genealogical, though often relatives of the deceased appear in the lists of debtors and creditors, but the inventory gives a vivid picture of the deceased's way of life. Unfortunately, this document is damaged and parts of it unreadable—

A True and perfect Inventory of all & singular the goods cattle & Chattels of William Barrett late of the Parish & Diocese of Mathon in the County of Worcester deceased taken and appraised the fifteenth day of February Ao: Dm 1703 by us whose names are hereunto subscribed as followeth

his money in purse & wearing apparrell	?	10	0
money owing by Speciality	?	10	0
money owing without speciality		?	
Corn	7	2	6
Brass of several sorts	1	6	0
Pewter of Several sorts	1	0	0
Linnen of Severall sorts	2	15	0
Blanketts & Coverlets	1	15	0
Three Bedds	6	0	0
Three Beddsteeds & one sett of Curtains	?	10	0
Two tables Two formes & one Cupboard	?	12	0
Fower Coffers & one Chest & Box		14	0
Cooppery ware of Severall sorts	2	5	0

Iron ware	1	12	0
Sheep fourty three	8	0	0
Lumber & other things not aforementioned		2	0
Grand totall	118	13	6

Unfortunately there are too many gaps to be able to fill in the values, but the sheep give an indication of relative prices —43 valued at £8; an average of about 3/9d. It will be noticed that there is brass, pewter, copper and ironware in the house, but no silver. No chairs are mentioned, though there are two forms and two tables.

Now another of William Barrett of the same parish taken on 2 May 1763, sixty years later than the first William—

In the kitchen Ten Pewter Dishes Eight Plates Twelve Patty pans a Pudding pan & Dripping pan One Spit three Candelsticks and Jack with its Implements One brass Kettle and frying pan three chairs a long Table & a form a fire piece	2	13	0
In the hall two Brass Kettles One bell mettle Pot an Iron do: three Chairs one Tin Dripping pan	1	1	6
In the Parlour One Feather Bed and Bolster four Blankets a pair of Sheets Bedsteed & hangings a round Table a large wheel & a small do: a Table Cloth & pair of Sheets	2	19	0
In a back Room three Tubbs a Kneading Stool one barrel		10	6
In the Room over the parlour one feather Bed & Bolster two Blankets & a pair of Bedsteeds two old Coffers one Chest two small Boxes two pair of Sheets	2	5	0
Wearing Apparrel	1	10	6
Money in purse	1	0	6
	12	0	0

Samuel Gwilliam
John Spencer } Apprs.

These show the nature of inventories and the kind of information that the genealogist finds in them : they bring us nearer to the men and women themselves than almost any other document, taking us into their houses, room by room, listing the contents. When attached to a detailed will, as is the case with the last inventory, we have both genealogy and background.

Chapter 5

HOLDING AND TRANSFER OF LAND

I N pre-Conquest days land was held in common, carved out of the forest and settled by small communities. Subjection, in return for protection, was the process whereby lords of the manor came into existence, protection being gradually taken over by the state as we now know it.

From becoming the absolute possession of the sovereign under the Normans, land gradually, until the nineteenth century, then rapidly, came under the absolute control of the occupier, or person who could show a good title to it. In more recent times, during this century, the freedom of the individual to do what he likes with his land has been reduced until now every change must first have the permission of the new lords of the manors—officials.

The genealogist, as he goes back across the years tracing the land of his ancestors, will be struck by the changing pattern of tenure, by the services demanded by the lord, by the duties of the customary tenant. But here we are dealing with the practical work of the searching genealogist, collecting information for his pedigree, trying to trace through the ownership of land the movement of his own family.

Probably he will have already discovered where they were living during the last hundred years, wills and parish registers will have tied the family down to certain districts. If he does not yet know the houses they actually occupied, he may be able to find out from old guides, or records of local landowners prepared for tax purposes. Which of these records are extant will be known by the local, or county, archivist. Enormous quantities of documents are available, as we saw at Headcorn—Highway Records, Rural District and Rating Documents, Poor Law Records, Borough Records, from which the searcher will be able to find out all the recent history of his family's lands. If he has access to solicitors' offices, or to local estate agents, he will have a further source of information, particularly where land belonged to large estates sold or developed from some central office, such as the estate office of the local lord. When he reaches documents which he cannot decypher, abbreviated latin, or Norman French, then he must come to terms with an archivist. More recent documents, during the last hundred, or two hundred, years, he should be able to decypher himself. Expense, as he might expect, increases as he goes back until he reaches the times when only experts can work, early manor rolls, for example, or Inquisitions Post Mortem, where not only are the terms abbreviated, but technical.

If the searcher has brought his pedigree back to, say, 1750, with wills, inventories and parish registers, he will find manor rolls the next step, filling gaps in wills and registers. They are hard to find, for they often lie far from the manors themselves. There is, for example, a wonderful set of Mathon in Worcestershire in the library at Westminster Abbey. Photocopies, when I examined them, were unknown; in any case the amount of information was so great that it would have been a great expense. Later, at the office of the Ecclesiastical Commissioners, I was shown a survey of 1798 with the tenants' holdings coloured, and a list of holders from approximately 1660-1800. There were also books of court proceedings from 1664 to about 1740, and further information about holders down to roughly 1860. Such finds are rare, not because these documents and books have been destroyed, but because they are hidden away and nobody knows about them.

MATHON MANOR HOLDERS Page 15. One messuage & one nook of land called Hedridges and the other nook of land and messuage called Thickletts and one piece of land called Woodland and one other messuage and nook of land called Sandridges with all the singular appurtenances. Quit Rent 16/8½d.
6 April 1683 Margaret James & William Randen in possession. William Randen jun Mary Randen & Thomas Randen in reversion.

12 Sept. 1710 William Randen in possession. Thomas Randen Thos. Dangerfield & Jno Dangerfield in reversion.

29 Aug. 1730 William Randen Elizabeth Randen Thomas Randen & William Randen jun in possession. William Meredith in reversion.

The records of this portion of the manor continue down to 1861, showing each change in possession as it occurred. Each piece of land is dealt with, and identified on the map. Then one comes across such useful records as this—

Mr. H. Dangerfield copyholder. Marshalls contains a farm house of a middling size part stone & brick in pannels & part timber framed & lath & plastered & whitewashed the roof part tiled & part Thatch'd now under repair. A hop kiln now building adjoining brick & tiled. A barn consisting of three bays timber fram'd & lath'd but middling.
A small stable & wain house part stone & brick and part boarded, thatch'd & in tight condition. A mill house & cow house part boarded & part lath'd, roof thatch'd in tolerable repair.
A lart hovel on posts thatch'd in middling plight. Annual value £47-14-6

Unfortunately there was no date, but I identified the property with Hill House. This may not be of use for the pedigree itself, but it shows the land living, changing, decaying, being renewed.

When we come to the court proceedings, we find the same kind of information, but presented differently—

September 1710 Sworn by the Homage that on 2 September William Randen Maria Stockton & Thomas Randen three customary tenants surrended out of court into the hands of Allain Randen & Henry Dangerfield Hedridges, Thickletts, Woodland & Sandridges & William Randen admitted tenant. Came Thomas Randen Thomas Dangerfield & John Dangerfield jun and became reversionary tenants on surrender of William Randen, tenant in possession.

On the surrendering and regranting of land there are many entries, for that was one of the principle functions of the court. Here is one, No. 8, on the court roll of August 1661 (abbreviated latin)—

Came Thomas Randen, Maria his wife and Maria his daughter and surrendered Parkers Close and Redfield which was given to them for life and Thomas admitted on payment of fine with Maria and Maria in reversion

When these entries, together with those of tenants doing homage at the courts, are matched up with parish registers and wills, it will be seen how complete a pedigree can be built up. Then, if the land can be identified from maps and a personal visit, the genealogist has not only his pedigree, but the material for a history.

A study of manor rolls, of course, leads the searcher into the organization of the manor, how manor courts were run, what was involved in surrender and regrant of land. One is led into a study of merchets and heriots, and the day-to-day running of the manor. In particular, though of little use to the pedigree, he will want to know the method of enforcing law and order, a subject which will be referred to later when we consider Patent and Close Rolls.

Chapter 6

COURT ROLLS, COPYHOLDERS, AND CHARTER ROLLS

L A N D was held in many different ways, and it is not possible to judge a man's social position by the way he held it. He could, for example, hold it freehold, leasehold, or copyhold, and be either rich or poor. We have the same situation today where some of our possessions are fully owned, others on hire-purchase, others may be rented. It make no difference to our social status.

Copyholders, particularly, are still identified in some minds with villeinage. But they, too, even in medieval times, were often substantial men, ranking close to those who held their land free. The copyholder had usually as much security as the freeholder, subject, of course, to complying with the customs of the manor. These varied from place to place, but it was possible to sue in the civil courts on the basis of the customs of the manor, and the lord was seldom the autocratic master he is made out. Among the records of Mathon, for example, is the following scrap of a legal dispute which refers for authority to the custom of the manor—

ROLL 21469

May 1548. At the same court held 22 April 1 Edward VI came William Bland, Agnes his wife and Elizabeth his daughter & claimed Hedges, Sandregs and Fyckeletts & Woodlands formerly held by Thomas Randen & Elizabeth his wife after litigation between Anne Randen daughter of said Thomas Randen and William Bland as set out below.

22 JAN 1 EDWARD VI
ANNE RANDEN COMPLT. V WILLIAM BLAND DEFT.
At which day Thomas Smythe attorney for the plaintiff

William Symonds and George Habynton gent (illegible, perhaps 'for the defendent') The plaintiff claims the messuages and lands as heir to her father Thomas Randen deceased according to the custom of the lordship of Mathon by her guardian which is that the issue and heir of any copyholder for term of life within the said lordship tendering like fine as their ancestors being but copyholders for term of life in time past paid ought by the said custom to enjoy the same lands as they their ancestors held by reason of the copies specially to them granted for time of life which custom is thought to this councell not allowable . . . (illegible) . . . and that the said defendant shall be dismissed out of this court with the possession of the land and the plaintiff finding her grieved to be at her remedy by the common law and the plaintiff to pay defendant 6/8d. costs and if the plantiff has sown any corn she to have the benefit thereof.

Here we see the local law by custom being enforced, and the strength of tenure by custom. The view of the copyholder as holding his land year by year at the mercy of his lord, working on the demesne land with plough and team, sweating out his life in menial service, is wrong. Certain kinds of tenure did certainly require personal service, sometimes in addition to payments in cash and kind, but over the centuries services were increasingly commuted. Men could not be held to the land, fines for leaving the manor soon became unenforcible; by the fourteenth century mobility of labour was accepted. The process was gradual, there was no one moment when feudal tenure ceased and the modern system of freehold and leasehold became universal, but sudden upheavals, such as the Black Death, strengthened the hand of the peasants and weakened the power of local lords.

If the genealogist finds his family occupying copyhold land, that does not mean that they were serfs : the lord of the manor may himself have been a copyholder of another manor. Nor does homage mean servitude : we are today as bound to mortgagors and building societies as were any of our ancestors to the manor.

If the searcher fails to find manor rolls, he may nevertheless find copies, the title deeds of the copyholder. These will, of course, be isolated documents and can never be a substitute for the original rolls; but they will establish who was tenant in possession, and perhaps in reversion, and be a valuable addition to and confirmation of parish registers and wills.

Often a public library collects manuscripts under some general title—'Miscellaneous MSS'—or under the name of the donor, such as the 'Cotton Collection'. These may contain manuscripts of all kinds, including manor rolls, and until each document is brought up it is sometimes impossible to know just from a card reference what it is. Indexing is usually being done on them, and it may be possible to pick out classes of records from the cards, but indexing is a long and expert task with old documents. If the searcher is lucky enough to find an *index nominum* he can then work through each reference taking the manuscripts as they come, marriage settlements, leases, transcripts of wills, copyholders' titles, or whatever they may be.

His disappointments will be many: he will sit waiting for what seemed a promising document, just the date he needs, the member of the family about whom he knows so little, but when it comes all he finds is the signature of a witness, the document itself being of no interest. Yet even that is not entirely useless, for the signature does at least establish that person living at that time and in that place. This may help subsequent searches, and where the name is common help to eliminate other members of the family.

But the greatest value of manor rolls is that they carry the family back far beyond the time of parish registers in a way that no other series of documents can. Families often tilled the same soil for generations, many families, once the searcher has passed beyond the Industrial Revolution, will be found settled generation by generation on the same manor for centuries. Some of these rolls go back to the thirteenth century, and if the searcher is lucky enough to find a complete series he could hardly spend his money better than in having a search made of such early ones as he cannot read himself.

Freeholders, of course, were not subject to the lord of the manor so their transfers were made independently of the courts. Thousands of charters exist, and these form a valuable source for the genealogist. The long series of Charter Rolls are as valuable as the Close and Patent Rolls, which will be considered later.

Outside the transcripts, of course, they do not appear in series, and the searcher is lucky to find extensive continuity, but they establish the land, tenant, and date, and are personal in a way that manor rolls never are. Originals may, moreover, bear signatures, although the ability to sign one's name was not universal even among gentry in earlier centuries.

When we come to enclosures, we cover another long period, for they were going on from earliest times, many disputes arising through rights of free grazing being encroached upon by the lord. The more general enclosure, the change from open farming to enclosed fields, gave rise less to disputes than to surveys, and though these are of more interest to someone writing a parish history than the history of a family, they can give detailed information about the family's holdings.

Occasionally, an Extent goes back to early times, such as those carried out by Burton Abbey, but these are isolated, and of limited value unless one's family happened to be one of the tenants at the time of the surveys.

Writing a family history differs fundamentally from writing a parish history. The parish historian focusses his inquiry on a narrow field, nothing beyond the parish boundaries interests him (except the setting of national events in which his parish history developed). The family historian, on the other hand, is interested in the whole country for he never knows where some branch of his family will turn up. As the volume of his material increases, he finds himself opening files for counties, he will have small pedigrees built up from one or two wills, or a few manor rolls, unable to fit that pedigree into anything else. He will find that the family appears to expand and contract over the centuries, sometimes full of male members splitting off and building their own branches. At other times he has these names on his pedigree and cannot find if they married, or when they died. Then, in some other part of the country, he finds that name occurring, perhaps in parish registers, but he cannot be sure if the two are the same, so he dare not enter the new family on the pedigree. In his searches he looks round everywhere, he never knows where he will find something : every journey an adventure, every library a treasure-house.

Chapter 7

INQUISITIONS POST MORTEM

WHEN a tenant *in capite* died, a writ *de diem clausit extremum* was sent to the escheator of the county in which he held land, or escheators of each county where he had extensive lands, requiring them to summon a jury and inquire what lands they were, by what service he held them, and the name and age of the heir. This was so that the king could claim wardship or other advantages due to him. If, for example, the heir was a minor, the king appointed a ward who managed his lands until such time as he could prove that he was of age.

Two series of documents exist, Chancery and Exchequer, the searcher often overcoming illegible or damaged parts of one document by referring to the other series. They cover the period Henry III to Charles I, approximately four hundred years, and provide information of great value to the genealogist. Calendars have been prepared, and the searcher is advised, after referring to Inquisitions listed under his own name, to turn to any holdings which were the subject of Inquisitions in the districts in which he is interested. Often a topographical search brings to light Inquisitions incorrectly indexed, the name misread, or even omitted. He may thus turn up a new spelling of his name, and from that be led to re-search old sources. In that way he finds new lands, and new branches of the family.

Most of the period covered by these Inquisitions is before parish registers and before wills became available in large numbers, so they are a valuable source for that period when the easily-reached sources are dying out. Genealogy consists in leaps, first one source is exhausted, then another; first living relatives, then parish registers, then wills, manor rolls, local collections, leases, mortgages; now we reach Inquisitions Post Mortem.

D

In practice, the genealogist is not so methodical. He does not completely exhaust one source before moving to the next. He makes whatever he can of parish registers, but he can never exhaust them; he keeps going back to them, or extending his range as new parishes are discovered. The leaps are taken in the process of building his pedigree, abandoning one source as it dies and taking another, moving back century by century.

Similarly with Inquisitions: he may find on first consulting them, that there are no apparent references to his family. Later, when he comes to the period before surnames were in general use, he may, and probably will, find his family using the topographical name, and he will then return to the whole field of Inquisitions, and to other sources, picking up information that, in his ignorance, he passed first time.

Here is an extract of a fifteenth century Inquisition to show the information derived from it—

JOHN EVOT—EXCHEQUER REFERENCE E/149/158/3

Inquisition taken at Maidstone, co. Kent, Friday after the feast of St. Cuthbert the Bishop, 14 Henry VI, before John Selby, the King's Escheator in the same County.

The jurors (named) say on oath that John Evot, named in the writ held no lands etc. in fee the day he died, but that a certain John Cle, Richard Amory, Robert Luton and Richard Orgare were seised of the third part of the manor of West branlyng als. Pympe in co. Kent and the same was held of the King in chief by the third part of a knight's fee and thus being seised with the King's licence, by deed of 12 March 6 Henry IV conveyed the same to a certain Thomas, son of William Evot late citizen and draper of London, and the heirs of his body to hold of the chief lords of the fee by the services accustomed, in default of such issue, contingent remainders to Robert, son of the said William Evot, and the heirs of his body, to William, son of the said William and the heirs of his body, to Margaret daughter of the said William the father and the heirs of her body, to Alice daughter, and the heirs of her body, to Margaret late the wife of the said William the father for her life, to John Evot, named in the writ, by the name of John, bastard son of the said William Evot the father and the heirs of his body, to William son of John Holden, of Hunton, co. Kent, and the heirs of his body, to Laurence, Thomas and Roger, sons of Bartholomew atte Wode, their heirs and assigns.

The jurors say that Thomas son of William Evot, late citizen and draper of London, Robert and William his other sons, Margaret and Alice his daughters, Margaret his wife, are all dead, his sons and daughters without issue, and after Margaret the wife's death, the said John Evot was seised of the same third part and died seised thereof in the vigil of St. Matthew the Apostle last past. The said third part is worth 4 marks clear yearly.

William son of John Holden of Hunton died in the lifetime of the said John Evot, without heir of his body as did likewise Laurence, son of Bartholomew atte Wode, and Thomas, son of Bartholomew atte Wode survives aged 50 years and more. Roger son of Bartholomew likewise died in the lifetime of the said John Evot having issue John, now surviving, aged 24 years and more.

The said John Evot had no heir because as is aforesaid the said John Evot was a bastard.

This document is packed with facts for the genealogist. The only thing it does not tell us is the relationship between John Evot and the families of Wode and Holden, and whether the deceased, John Evot, had any heirs. As a bastard, land could not pass through him, but that does not mean that he d.s.p. Nevertheless, it gives a detailed record of one generation.

It is impossible to say whether this branch of the family died out until it is known whether John Evot left issue, but if he did he was the only member of that generation to do so. The other issue of William the father, male and female, all d.s.p.

In this particular case the branch was an isolated one that only came to light after a search of the calendars of Inquisitions. Until then there had been no information about them.

THE FAMILY OF EVOT

WILLIAM EVOT = MARGARET
citizen & draper of | alive 1405 d.
London d. before 1436 | before 1436

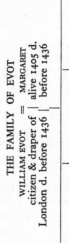

THOMAS EVOT	ROBERT EVOT	WILLIAM EVOT	MARGARET EVOT	ALICE EVOT
alive 1405	alive 1405	alive 1405	alive 1405	alive 1405
dsp. before 1436	dsp. before 1436	dsp. before 1436	dsp. before 1436	dsp. before 1436

JOHN EVOT
(base son)
½ manor of
West Barming
d. 1435/6 I.P.M.
E/149/158/3

THE FAMILIES OF HOLDEN AND ATTE WODE

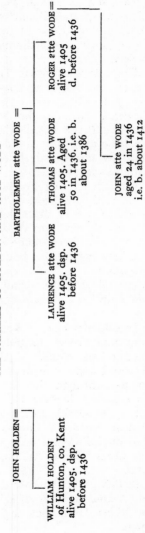

BARTHOLEMEW atte WODE =

JOHN HOLDEN =

LAURENCE atte WODE	THOMAS atte WODE	ROGER atte WODE =
alive 1405. dsp.	alive 1405. Aged	alive 1405
before 1436	50 in 1436. i.e. b.	d. before 1436
	about 1386	

WILLIAM HOLDEN
of Hunton, co. Kent
alive 1405. dsp.
before 1436

JOHN atte WODE
aged 24 in 1436
i.e. b. about 1412

As the reader will realize, a new territory is opened up by this single document: a series of questions arise, among which the following—

1. Did John Evot have land in any other county besides Kent, and was an Inquitition held under some other name (Evot is not a usual name, and may be a misreading)?

2. Where did William, the father, obtain the third part of the manor? If by inheritance, there may be earlier Inquisitions, therefore a search is necessary under the manor as well as the name.

3. Do any manor rolls exist for West bramlyng (Barming)?

4. Are there any entries in the Fine, Patent, or Close Rolls concerned with the descent of the manor?

5. Tracing back the families of atte Wode and Holden might give a common ancestor and thus show where William the father came from.

One question raises another, hours of work are opened up by this single Inquisition. As it happens, the wills of both John Evot and his father William were proved in the P.C.C. (John Evot's given earlier). They give valuable information about the kind of people they were, and add many other questions to those above, introducing other land possessed by William the father, and extending the search to London. So the net widens, the unanswered questions multiply, and as they are answered the pedigree grows in extent and richness. It may be years before the genealogist can settle down to this branch of the family, and for those years the pedigree remains in his file. Then perhaps his main pedigree has a William for whom he cannot account, born in the middle of the fourteenth century, of whose marriage he has no record, nor of his death, nor issue. He remembers this William, and sets about trying to establish that they are the same.

He may, for example, be able to trace him through the records of the Drapers' Company, through apprenticeship, perhaps. It may be necessary to trace through in detail the manor of West Barming to find when it was split into three, though it may be found, at the end of a long search, that William Evot obtained it by purchase. Another avenue of search would be to take the trustees, John Cle, Richard Amory, Robert Luton and Richard Orgare, and find if they appear in other enfeoffments. There are many errors in names, and they may bring out further references overlooked in the earlier search.

Chapter 8

INQUISITIONS AD QUOD DAMNUM

J U S T as Inquisitions Post Mortem were held to see if the king's rights were affected by the death of a tenant, so other rights might be endangered when applications were made to alienate land, or for the grant of a market or fair. A writ was again issued to the local sheriff, or escheator, and the Inquisition was held and a report made as to the effect on the revenue of granting the request. If, for example, it was to transfer land to the church, that might deprive the king of revenue because it put an end to subsequent transfers, and therefore to subsequent fines. There could never again be a wardship on the minority of an heir, and on granting rights of holding a market or fair, it might encroach on a royal manor, or give benefits to a local landowner at the expense of the crown.

To the genealogist, the value of these Inquisitions is less than that of Inquisitions Post Mortem, and sometimes they turn out to be of no value, yet they are a necessary source of information and should at some stage be covered in the general search.

One of their subsidiary values is that they often lead to a subsequent charter, or licence to alienate in mortmain (to a monastery, chantry, or other 'dead hand'), and so introduce the searcher to another source of information. If, for example, he finds that the Inquisition reported no harm to the king by the proposed grant, he can then search the Charter Rolls.

The following is taken from Historical Collections: Staffordshire, Vol. 1911 p. 329, giving details not only of the land but of those concerned in the Inquisition—

KINVER MANOR. 9 Edw. II
An Inquisition made before the King's Escheator, at Kynne-

fare the 23rd day of May in the 9th Edw. II (1316), viz., whether or not it will be to the damage or prejudice of the King, or of any other person, if the King grant to Richard son of Bertram de Pickethorn, and Bertram his brother, that they may retain and have to themselves and their heirs, by the services thereof due and accustomed, two acres and two roods and a half of meadow in Kynnefare, which they acquire in fee to themselves and their heirs, from John de la Lee of Bobynton, who held them of the King in chief, without having attained the King's licence thereof: by the oath of William Attelowe, Gilbert de Duntesleye, John the clerk, John atte Birches, William de Follbrok (Phillibrook), John de Beumes, Edmund de Evenfeld, Benedict de Nolfeld, and Henry atte Place (?Pute), William Roulf, Richard Milehull, and Adam Blakeleye: who say upon their oath, that it will not be to the damage or prejudice of the King, nor of any other person, if the Lord the King grant to Richard son of Bertram de Picke- thorn, etc., and they say that the aforesaid land is holden of the King in chief, by the service of fourteen pence yearly, and it is worth by the year in all issues 2s. beyond the service aforesaid: and they say that certain lands and tenements will remain to the same John, beyond the said meadow, in the County of Stafford: and they are holden of Hugh de Hepham, Lord of Bobynton, by the service of 6s. 8d. yearly: and they are worth yearly in all issues 40s.

In witness whereof, etc.

When these great series of documents are inspected— Inquisitions, Close Rolls, Fine Rolls, and the others—the searcher will inevitably find much material that he cannot immediately fit into his pedigree. It may be years before he can work it back sufficiently far to include even those of, say, the fourteenth century. In the meantime, the information is filed until there is enough from that and other sources for the genealogist to concentrate on that period and make a systematic search of all the records. Admittedly, going to each source many times, covering closely only the period in which he happens at the time to be interested, increases the work.

But he will in any case make many journeys to the Inquisitions, as well as to most other sources, for, as we have seen, he continually extends his range with new names, and new places.

Those living in London have the best facilities, for not only are the great collections there—Somerset House, Record Office, British Museum—but he can find easily these indexes and printed volumes which, in the provinces, are only available in the largest libraries. Most county towns now have Charter, Fine, Close and Patent Rolls, either in their city, or county, libraries, but they cannot hold all the indexes of all the series. Many, for example, are in manuscript, no copies existing other than those in London.

The country genealogist, therefore, is restricted, and he may have to employ professional searchers for work that, if he was in London, he could do himself. And not only do himself without cost, but do better, for no one employed professionally can find those unexpected treasures. A professional makes the specific search ordered by his client, searching, say, Inquisitions ad Quod Damnum for a certain period under a certain name, but the searcher himself, going through the indexes, often sees a reference that looks promising, and in that way makes some of his happiest discoveries. It is really a question of involvement. The professional searcher is not involved, there is nothing in him of those whom he records, no warmth, no pride.

Not every Inquisition ad Quod Damnum was specifically to find out whether any damage would be done to the king. Some were of a more general character, connected with a possible alienation of land, but often general inquiries in the course of the financial administration of the king's land and the carrying out of his duties. Here are some, taken also from the Historical Collections: Staffordshire Vol. 1911—

TETTENHALL, Royal Domain. 33 Hen. III

Writ addressed to the Sheriff of Staffordshire to make an Extent of the Manor of Tetenhall, as to its worth by the year

in demesnes, villeinages, rents, escheats, and other profits—
Westminster, 24 October (1249)

ROB. de BOREWEY—Felon. 34 Hen. III

Writ to the Sheriff of Staffordshire to inquire whether one
messuage and six acres of land which Robert de Boreweya
(who was outlawed for felony) held in Rydeware Hamestal,
have been in the King's hands for one year and a day, and of
whom that messuage and land are holden—Westminster,
18 October (1250)

CROXTON ABBEY. 35 Hen. III

Writ addressed to the Sheriff of Staffordshire to inquire
what liberties the Abbot and Convent of Crockesden have by
Royal Charter from the King's predecessors, and what articles
of the same liberties they still use, and in what manner they
are used, and by whom—Nottingham, 25 November (1250)

Other kinds of Inquisitions were also held, collected under
the headings of Criminal and Miscellaneous, and the searcher
will no doubt cover them all when he deals with this important source. If he is pressed for time, or feels unable to deal
with the original documents, he can carry out the initial
search of the indexes, listing such entries as look useful, thus
doing at least part of the work himself, selecting those he
thinks valuable enough to pass over to an expert. He will
probably find when he reaches the thirteenth and fourteenth
centuries, that searches under places will be better than under
names, and he may have to postpone searching all these early
Inquisitions until he knows where his family lived in that
period. Without that, of course, he can only search under the
name, and that may lead him to much fruitless work if his
name is common.

Chapter 9

MARRIAGE SETTLEMENTS

T H E S E have been favoured by certain classes of society for centuries, and are still common in our own day. They were usually made in anticipation of marriage, some wording such as: 'there is a marriage agreed upon and shortly to be solemnized', being inserted so as to define its purpose. Sometimes it was not drawn up until after the marriage, in which case one finds: 'recently solemnized', or other equivalent phrase. Often the father of the bride, for his part, paid the dowry in cash, the intending husband making the settlement on himself, then on his wife, then on any issue of the marriage.

The value to the genealogist is mainly in the list of property coming under the settlement for it gives an accurate picture of their wealth, and often an indication of the status of both parties. Some of these documents are of great length, bolster-like, with precise descriptions of the land settled, sometimes leading the searcher to parts of the country where he finds another branch of the family. The issue of the marriage, for example, might spread over the different properties, and the fate of a younger son, previously lost, might thereby be traced. He will, in any case, trace the land until it passes out of the family, and in the process is sure to learn much of interest.

Apart from the property, of course, there are the parties to the settlement, and these often give information about the bride's family which may not be available from any other source. Here, for example, is one from the Local Collection at Hereford City Library, a long document in 20 parts, of which the following is an extract of Part 6—

27 August 1723 Indenture between Robert Holmes of Birchen co. Hereford Esquire of the first part, Joyce Webb of Barton-

street co. Gloucester widow of the second part, Francis
Brydges of the city of Hereford Esquire of the third part, and
John Cocks of the city of Gloucester Esquire, Edmund
Chamberlayn of Mangesbury co. Gloucester Esquire, Robert
Cocks gentleman one of the sons of Rev. Dr. Cocks of Wood-
stock co. Oxford and Edward James of the city of Gloucester
gentleman of fourth part WHEREAS there is a marriage agreed
upon and shortly to be solemnised between Robert Holmes
and Joyce Webb AND WHEREAS Robert Holmes being seised
of a very considerable estate in lands and tenements in the
said county of Hereford and the said Joyce Webb by virtue as
well of her jointure made upon her marriage with Nicholas
Webb Esquire her late husband dated as by his last will and
testament and otherwise is also seised and possessed of a very
considerable estate in lands and also possessed of and well
entitled to a very large personal estate consisting of chattle
leases goods and household goods ready monies and securities
for money in bonds bills mortgage notes and contracts THEN
THE SAID Robert Holmes and Joyce Webb have agreed THAT
HE WILL settle a sufficient part of his estate to provide £200
per annum free of tax for the said Joyce Webb AND THAT
SHE WILL CONVEY to the said Francis Brydges (Here follow
the properties respectively settled by each of the parties) . . .

This sets out not only Robert Holmes's property, but that
of his intending wife. There is, it is true, no indication of the
age of the two parties, and one cannot tell whether it was the
first marriage of Robert Holmes. As it happens, from other
sources, he is known to have been married before, and that
he married a third time after the death of Joyce Webb. But
it was she who bore his children, and through this marriage
settlement the property descended to them.

There is no room here to set out the property, but the
searcher would find many new directions in which to look,
and when he had exhausted them he could turn to the other
parties to the settlement, the trustees, and by consulting
records concerning them perhaps collect other facts about the
principle parties. Such searches, of course, as they move away

from the family, become progressively less useful. One might, for example, examine many documents of Brydges, Cocks and Chamberlayn without finding any mention of Joyce Webb. But they are avenues of search if some important piece of evidence is missing and can be found no other way. Their wills, for example, could be searched without great trouble.

Once again one comes against searches of the female line, wondering how far to go with them. One is naturally interested, if making a pedigree of the family of Holmes, to find out who Joyce Webb's father was, and perhaps something about her first husband. But there comes a point beyond which one cannot pass without moving right outside the family with which one is directly concerned.

Marriage settlements were not confined to the gentry. Here is one of a yeoman of the seventeenth century, connected, as has been established from other sources, with the later Robert Holmes—

20 July 1667 between Richard Hooper of Ashperton yeoman of the first part, John Holmes of Collwall yeoman of the second part, Nicholas Phillpott the younger of Marden gentleman and Morgan Morgan of the city of Hereford gentleman of the third part, and Richard Skyrme the younger of the city of Hereford and Thomas Dangerfield of Collwall gentleman of the fourth part WITNESSETH that the said Richard Hooper in consideration of a marriage already solemnised between the said John Holmes and Frances his now wife one of the daughters of the said Richard Hooper and in consideration of money paid by John Holmes he transfers to Nicholas Phillpott and Morgan Morgan that messuage called the Deykynhouse and five acres of land, and nine acres in a field called Haywood field adjoining the aforementioned closes formerly in tenure of Richard Seycell deceased, and that decayed messuage with two acres, and four acres in Leafield (and other land specified) and land purchased by Richard Hooper of Walter Hopton Esquire, and the decayed cottage called the Lesser Cottage heretofore in the possession of Thomas Harton with the half-acre purchased of Jane Baggard, and two acres

in Longerland field purchased of James Godsall all in the parish
of Ashperton TO HAVE AND TO HOLD FOR THE FOLLOW-
ING USES—the two acres purchased of James Godsall for the
use of the said John Holmes the rest to Richard Hooper and
Frances his wife for life then to John Holmes and Frances his
wife and their issue who failing to the heirs of Richard Hooper.
(Reference also to a mortgage dated 7 August 1657 by Richard
Hooper to Robert Pytt of part of the said premises securing
£110 to the said Robert Pytt within six months of decease of
Richard Hooper)
Signed by Rich Hoop (sic). The marks of John Holmes,
Nicholas Phillpott, Mor. Morgan, Ri Skyrme, Thomas Danger-
field.

From this it will be seen that it is the father-in-law who
settles the land, and that the settlement was made after
marriage, though there is no way of knowing from this settlement how long after. But it opens up the two parishes of
Collwall and Ashperton, and there may be records of the
marriage and of issue baptized in one or other of the parishes.
From that one would find out in which of them they settled.
Richard Hooper was evidently one of these prosperous yeomen, on the borderline of yeoman/gentleman. A search of the
wills of Richard Hooper and his wife Frances might give
additional information of any issue to John Holmes and
Frances. The pedigree from the settlement is as follows—

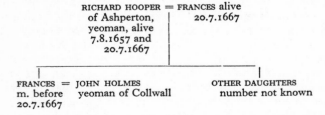

The use one can make of this information depends, of course,
on the stage of one's search. It may give the final information
on a section of the pedigree already almost complete, serving

to confirm what is already known rather than to bring in something new. On Richard Hooper's personal sheet there may already be a list of his children, the only missing detail being perhaps what happened to his daughter Frances. In that case, he enters her marriage to John Holmes, sometime before 20 July 1667, and if he is only following the male line of the Hoopers the pedigree will end there.

Or this may be something entirely new, discovered only when he went through the index and called for the document. What he does then depends on whether he can fit this new member of the family into the pedigree. He may, for example, already have a Richard Hooper married to a wife Frances, but no trace of where he lived. This may place him at Ashperton and so cause him to examine the parish registers and start building up information about this hitherto unknown member of the family. If he finds that their only issue were Frances, who married John Holmes, and other daughters, no male issue, then that branch of the family can be left from the point of view of the continuance of the surname. Another section of the pedigree is thus ended, and he turns to some other male issue to continue his search.

If, on the other hand, he does not know whose son Richard Hooper was, he must go back until he can link him to the pedigree. He will search the parish registers, year by year, looking for any entries of Hoopers, his marriage perhaps, even his baptism. If he was baptized at Ashperton, then perhaps his father held land there, so the registers are covered right back to the beginning. Perhaps there is no record of either marriage or baptisms. How did he come into that land? He searches other parish registers, wills at the local depository, or wherever he thinks they may be found (perhaps at Worcester). He keeps driving back, tracing previous owners of the land, through Inquisitions Post Mortem, the usual searches we have already considered, back until he can fasten Richard Hooper on to the pedigree.

He may stay unattached for years, just a glimpse of a generation, living, marrying, settling their land; an isolated family with no past, the surname dying out in the second generation. Years later, another grain of information may be found, another direction given to the search, another link discovered, perhaps a leap backwards to the junction.

There are, of course, many sources to search besides those mentioned, as will be seen in later chapters, but in genealogy these members of the family about whom nothing is known are constantly being discovered, and the genealogist soon finds himself with many clusters, like that of Richard Hooper, growing as each additional piece is added, until they seem ripe for that final addition that makes them fall into place.

If, on the other hand, one was searching under Holmes, the inquiry would continue both back and forward. One would want to know, if one did not already know, where he came from, and whether he had issue by Frances Hooper. The search would cover the same ground only would go in both directions. He may have farmed the land in both parishes, though they are several miles apart, and the first search would probably be to find out where he died and so tie him down physically to one parish or the other. Then there would be the usual search of manor rolls, leases, wills : the pattern of each search is the same.

There is not, so far as I know, any special place to find marriage settlements. They are personal documents, not collected into national depositories. Local collections in city libraries are the most likely places, or the offices of solicitors. The value of old documents is gradually being recognized; slowly they are finding their way into public custody for the benefit of the general searcher. Because there is nothing in the index today, it does not mean that there will be nothing tomorrow.

Chapter 10

CHARTERS AND LEASES

M E N T I O N was made earlier of the method of transferring land by charters and leases as opposed to that of surrender and readmission under the copyhold system. Like marriage settlements, charters and leases are mainly to be found among the miscellaneous collections at libraries and will be covered during the genealogist's search of local sources. Perhaps, where the numbers are considerable, they may be separately indexed, but usually these local collections contain too many different kinds for each to be separately indexed. He may therefore find, as he works through the index, all manner of documents coming forward, among them these leases and charters.

Here is one of the fifteenth century from the Hopton Collection at Hereford City Library—

Know (all men) present and to come that I William Herthe formerly of Castlefrome have given, granted and by this my present charter have confirmed to Thomas Arundell the elder and Thomas Arundell his son, all my lands and tenements, rents and services with meadows, pastures, right of pasture, woods and their appurtenances lying in Castlefrome aforesaid called Morehendisland which formerly were (the property) of John de Morehende, to have and to hold all the said lands and tenements, rents and services with meadows, pastures, right of pasture, woods and their appurtenances to the said Thomas Arundell the elder and Thomas his son, their heirs and assigns for ever, of the chief lord of the fees for services owing to them and by right accustomed. And I the said William Herthe and my heirs will warrant and defend against all men forever all the said lands and tenements, rents and services with meadows, pastures, right of pasture, woods and their appurtenances to the said Thomas Arundell the elder and Thomas his

E

son, their heirs and assigns. In testimony of which things I
have placed by seal on this my present charter. With these
witnesses (here named). Given at Castlefrome the third day
of the month of May in the year of the reign of King Henry VI
after the Conquest, 25 (1447)

This is a simple, straightforward document. Not much information can be gathered from it beyond the existence at that
date of Thomas Arundell and his son Thomas, together with
the names of the transferor and witnesses. Yet even the date,
and the fact of those persons being alive, may provide some
genealogist with valuable information. If, on the other hand,
the property itself, Morehendisland, is the subject of the inquiry, then it provides proof of its descent at that period and
may be the link which the searcher needs.

It is not possible to tell whether the land in question took
its name from the previous owner, John de Morehende, or
whether the land was always called that and John took his
name from it. Identification of people by property was
common even as late as that, and it may be that John's family
name was different, he being identified in this instance as 'de
Morehende' and perhaps at the same time elsewhere as John
de Hereford, or John de Gloucester. We are, however, fortunate in having the main people in this transfer clearly
identified under the surnames of Herthe and Arundell.

Witnesses to a document are often informative, for those
who signed first were the most important, either as regards
the property transferred, or in relation to the parties concerned. The first witness might be the lord of the manor near
which the land lies, or the person to whom services are due,
the above land being held 'of the chief lord of the fees for
services owing to them and by right accustomed'. When
making extracts, at least the first few witnesses should be
noted, though those near the end, for there are often many,
are less important. A dozen witnesses is not uncommon, the
number increasing as the years go back.

Charters are some of the earliest documents existing; many
of the Saxon period have survived and are collected as

'Cartularies'. I do not propose to deal with those because they mostly date to a period earlier than the genealogist for whom this book is written will cover. He is more interested in the series of Charter Rolls at the Record Office, transfers of land within the period of his pedigree enabling him to fill in details of his own family. By the time he has worked back to the early centuries, he will have enough experience to find and examine these earliest charters. They are, in any case, often disappointing. Seldom can an individual be positively identified owing to the lack of surnames, and often when the document is produced we have no more than the name of a witness. The searcher may find in his files many possible ancestors of Norman, or even Saxon, days, but with no hope of being able to fit them into a pedigree.

Yet a great value of early charters is that they locate a family. Every pedigree, as it is worked back, reaches a point beyond which the searcher cannot go. He searches the usual places, but finds nothing of interest, he does not know where the first person came from, whether he was born where he is known to be, or whether he moved there from somewhere else. There is no record of anyone earlier, not even casual names showing continuity of tenure. Charters can direct the searcher to new localities and open up the pedigree again.

But, as with all early sources, there are gaps, particularly when he is in the Norman or pre-Norman period. He will be fortunate if he finds more than isolated references to people whom he can with some certainty identify with his own family. Genuine pedigrees back to the Conquest are very rare.

When it comes to official. or semi-official, bodies, if one may so describe monastries and boroughs in the old days, it was the practice to copy charters into registers and many of these have been preserved. They are not, of course, original documents, but in their absence the copies can be accepted, indeed, they must be, for there is rarely any confirmation. There is a difference between using such information and accepting facts collected by more modern writers for perhaps other purposes.

Amateurs sometimes write their family histories, have them

privately printed, and so they come on the market. But they may contain mistakes, extracts taken from documents for the special purpose of that family omitting other facts that did not happen to interest that particular searcher. Sometimes assumptions are made not warranted by the facts, the pedigree containing information that has not been verified. Such books are treated by the searcher with reserve, he goes back always to the source, inevitably covering the same ground and perhaps arriving at no different conclusion, but occasionally avoiding some important mistake that would have thrown out his pedigree.

With transcripts of early charters, however, he has no choice; the originals have long since disappeared. Nor is there the same danger, for copies were made for reference and no doubt every effort was made to have them exact. It is a different problem from that of the modern amateur.

Here is a late-seventeenth century lease giving more genealogical information than usual—

22 February 1697 between Michael Lorimer of the parish of St. Martin's London, citizen & haberdasher, son and heir apparent of William Lorimer late of Bosbury co. Hereford gentleman deceased who was grandson and heir of Edward Lorimer late of Bosbury gentleman deceased of the first part, and Francis Brydges of the city of Hereford Esquire of the other part WITNESSETH that he the said Michael Lorimer in consideration of five shillings hath leased three acres of land called Hemey and land in the Manor of Upleadon called Temple Court in the parish of Bosbury heretofore held by the said Edward Lorimer great grandfather of the said Michael Lorimer, for one year at a peppercorn rent.

This gives the following Lorimer pedigree—

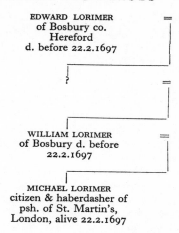

EDWARD LORIMER
of Bosbury co.
Hereford
d. before 22.2.1697

WILLIAM LORIMER
of Bosbury d. before
22.2.1697

MICHAEL LORIMER
citizen & haberdasher of
psh. of St. Martin's,
London, alive 22.2.1697

It is unusual to obtain such detailed information covering four generations. It will be noted that the great grandfather is shown as having 'd. before 22.2.1697'. This is unavoidably vague, for he may have died many years before, but it is the only fact of which we can be sure. In a pedigree there is all the difference between 'died before . . .', and 'died about . . .'.

The description of Michael Lorimer as 'son and heir apparent of William Lorimer late of Bosbury co. Hereford gentleman deceased' is perhaps confusing. It is clear that William Lorimer the father is dead, but not clear why Michael is described as heir 'apparent'. It is possible that this document was signed so soon after his father's death that it was thought advisable to make that reservation, but all we can put in the pedigree is that William was dead. A search of the parish registers would clear it up.

It also looks as if the great grandfather held Temple Court long enough to pass it direct to his grandson, William. His son (name not given) perhaps predeceased his father. Again, the registers at Bosbury will fill the gaps. If not, there may be manor rolls of Upleadon Manor, or local wills to fill in.

As it happens, these sources have been searched and the gaps have been filled and the pedigree completed and joined to the main pedigree, but only the limited information given above can be arrived at directly from the lease.

Here is a lease that helps the local historian, giving him information about the situation of land and the holders of it—

27 September 1701 between the mayor and aldermen of the city of Hereford and Richard Thompson of the parish of Castle Frome gentleman WITNESSETH that for £30 received have let unto the said Richard Thompson their Barne called the Marsh Barn being 70 feet in length in the parish of Much Cowarne with the fould or yard belonging and also 2½ acres of pasture in a place called Hill End in the parish of Much Cowarne between lands of Richard Berrington gentleman now in the occupation of Richard Burfoote on one part and the King's highway on the other part and land and meadow near Perry Field and one acre of land in Richloe Field and much other land (specified) for 21 years @ £3 p.a.

Finally, here is an extract of a lease showing the kind of terms common in the eighteenth century between a lord and his tenant—

10 June 1749 between Robert Thompson of Castle Frome Esquire of the first part Edward Bourn the younger of Castle Frome yeoman and Martha his wife and Edward their son of the other part WITNESSETH that Robert Thompson, for £30, leases certain lands (specified) @ 10 shillings a year and one couple of good fat live capons or a good fat live goose (at the choice of the landlord) on 26 December yearly and they shall plant two apple trees or pear trees until the land is sufficiently filled up. On the lease is an endorsement (unsigned) stating that the lease was surrendered Febr. 2 1807 in consideration of £160 paid by Edwd. Poole to John Bourne.

At the present time we have ground rents whereby a landlord leases for a long term, sometimes in perpetuity, land for development on the understanding that the land, when the lease expires, shall revert to the original owner together with any buildings that may have been erected on it. If the lease is for, say, 999 years, the tenure may be considered freehold, subject of course, to the payment of the ground rent. There are now, as there always have been, many kinds of tenure. There is no reason why two people today should not come to an agreement similar to that of 1749 if they wished. One cannot, for example, assume that every tenant on a manor was treated alike; tenure extended from that of tenants in chief holding direct from the king, through the relative security of middle-class tenures, down to the precarious existence of a bondman.

Chapter 11

LAW AND ADMINISTRATION

W E have been dealing with comparatively small classes of records—Inquisitions, parish registers, wills—most of them found in local depositories and probably not taking more than a few weeks to inspect. Now we come to the great classes of records preserved at the Record Office covering in some cases hundreds of years, each giving a pattern of life continuously for the whole country, stretching back far enough almost to link up with Domesday Book.

These, it is true, can be examined for particular periods, whatever period the searcher is working on, but it is usually better to search the whole series, even though later, as new material comes to light, further reference is needed. Most large provincial libraries have copies of these calendars, or at least of the indexes, and from these the originals in London can be examined. There are, in addition to the Charter Rolls, the Close Rolls, Patent Rolls, Fine Rolls, Pipe Rolls, Plea Rolls, and others which will be dealt with in turn. Here we will consider Law and Administration, civil and criminal, which form the basis of these documents, dealing also, briefly, with ecclesiastical discipline, then with the records of Chancery Proceedings.

Justice, in early times, was dispensed locally. As roads were bad, travelling often dangerous, few bridges, mud tracks through the forests, each village lived its self-contained life isolated and often unaware of events taking place in other parts of the country. The local lord, sheriff, or, later, escheator, governed on behalf of the king. It would have been impossible to refer every dispute to London, partly because of the difficulties of communication, also because the king and chief officers of state frequently moved about the country, there being no permanent seat of justice as we have it today.

Lords of manors often had great power, even that of death, and the system of communal responsibility for acts committed on the manor, or within defined areas, was common. No doubt this led to injustice, a tyrannical lord could act viciously : but not all lords were vicious, and on many manors the reeve and his council of tenants had more power than the lord.

No doubt the quality of justice varied from manor to manor, and changed to at least some extent as one lord inherited from another. But an advantage was that a man was tried in the place where his crime was committed, by people who knew him. The punishment was also local, and, more than today, the personal concern of those living near. Today it is impersonal, often as if the letter of the law mattered more than the crime; the dignity of office more than the heart. Today, also, punishment is more savage. We have the press, more heartless than any manor court, spreading the criminal's name not only among the few who saw him in the local stocks, but to the whole country. Today a man must cross the sea, change his name, and hope not to be recognized. Crimes dealt with in the manor court, or, where appropriate in the ecclesiastical court, were handled in a more humane manner, and certainly were more personal.

When, however, we consider free men, not subject to the lord of the manor, we find justice dispensed in itinerant courts, taking us to the records of Quarter Sessions, Assizes, and finally to the courts of Chancery. Lawyers drew a line between free and non-free (a line sometimes hard to draw for a bondman in one part of the country might be free in another). There was no national level of justice by which all men were judged, there was one system for the free, one for the non-free. The villein, in early days, was the possession of his lord. At his death his property reverted to the lord, and his heir had to pay a fine to retain it. Yet the movement was always towards equality. We find villeins soon after the Conquest coming to terms with their lords, even bargaining over their rights. This is not the act of slaves.

Such matters, however, are not of direct concern to the

genealogist, though he cannot avoid being to some extent drawn into the history of the times. For not only does he find his files filled with uncompleted searches, but his knowledge is widening, new subjects are learned, things he never thought about before—penalties in the Middle Ages for sheep stealing, or murder, or enclosure of common land. fines for overcharging for beer, or giving underweight of bread, for trespass, or excessive tolls. Unattached pedigrees lie in his files, and unexplored subjects lie in his mind.

It is easy to oversimplify the problems to state that a villein was dealt with in the manor court, and a free man by itinerant judges. It is still easier to class all those who gave service to their lord as villeins, and others, who had compounded, as free. But such clear distinctions are not valid. Only on an ideal manor could such a rule apply, where the demesne was compact so that the tenants could work it easily, where supervision by the reeve or steward was effective, and where obligations could be precisely enforced. But many manors covered great areas of wild country, the demesne might consist of land that could be better cultivated by hired labour. In time, a tenant who had commuted his services would consider himself free, particularly when his fines were fixed for ever. Yet basically the tenure was still service, moving first to tenure without a copy of the court roll (*custumarius sine copia*), finally to tenure with a copy—copyhold.

Even when service in kind was given, there were differences. The service of accompanying the lord on his hunting expeditions was clearly more honourable than carting manure for some obscure lord on a half-derelict manor. There was a striving upwards, from one form of service to another: the common man could become a gentleman; the gentleman an esquire; the esquire a knight.

The gradual emancipation of the villein automatically affected his legal rights, so that it is hard for a genealogist to know where he may find records of his own family. He cannot say that as freemen, for example, he will find nothing in manor rolls, for branches of the family may well have been bondmen. He has no real option but to search all the records, much of it unavoidably fruitless. Also he has to remember that a freeman may hold land by villein tenure. That does not make him a villein, though in respect of that part of his land he is liable to the service of villeinage tenure. So it does not follow that a freeman never has recourse to a manor court, nor that a villein appearing in a manor court may not also hold land as a freeman. Villeinage was a system of tenure, not a social class, degrees of bondage and freedom varying, merging into each other, one man holding land in many ways, subject to jurisdiction in several courts, yet still basically free.

Again, the genealogist may feel that all he is concerned with is that a certain member of his family was, perhaps, fined for allowing his cattle to stray, or had to pay a merchet for his daughter to marry off the manor, or to pay a heriot to take over on his father's death. These are facts that he can enter on his pedigree; he need not be involved in the intricacies of manorial customs.

Yet one thing leads to another: he may come across a merchet and not be sure what it is. He looks it up, and finds himself inside that manor, wondering what form the fine took, if it was a beast, what kind of beast, in what condition, of what value. He may find that someone on his pedigree paid a capon a year to live off the manor, or a large sum to leave the manor for life: he wonders why they went, whether to leave trouble behind, or because there was more attractive work in a nearby town. The bare facts are necessary, of course, but they are sometimes so bare that the searcher must clothe them with the mantle of the time.

Chapter 12

ECCLESIASTICAL ADMINISTRATION
AND RECORDS

W H E N we examine records of manor courts and find Views of Frankpledge, or meetings of the tithings, we know what was happening. From the mention of a name we have some idea of the position of that person in the community, how, for example, he was subject to civil rather than to ecclesiastical authority. When we come to the period before parish registers and wills, we may find traces of humble ancestors only in the disciplinary records. Unless a man was summoned as a tithing member, or perhaps himself on trial for allowing his sheep to stray, or otherwise offending against the laws of the manor, we have no record of his existence. The rest of his life, birth, marriage and death, pass unrecorded. Of course, this gives a distorted view of his life: one single crime does not make a man a criminal.

Many of the early records of a family, however, are of penalties. As a result, we are apt to over-emphasize the lawlessness of the times, assuming that people lived in constant trouble, always assaulting each other, defrauding each other of their lawful possessions. We forget the years they spent working on their land, quietly carrying out their obligations to their lord, worshipping at the parish church, gathering wood, making and repairing farm implements. We only see them facing the law, paying fines, going to prison. We picture their life as all crime and punishment.

For freemen, as opposed to villeins, the principle penalty was confiscation of land by the crown. We have seen under the Inquisitions ad Quod Damnum that the king was interested in all the land of the realm. Forfeiture was the penalty paid by tenants in chief, the king retaining the revenues sometimes for several years before either restoring the land, or giving it to someone else. A bondman, all of whose possessions legally belonged to his lord, had nothing to offer but his services, he had nothing to confiscate; but the lord himself had the land itself. The Saxon thegn's land was confiscated by the Norman invader, not in that case because of crime but through the process of military conquest. But confiscation continued as punishment.

Collective fines were common in Norman times, the responsibility of a number of men for each other being the basis of rural law and order. The View of Frankpledge ensured that collective responsibility functioned, and it has been extending over the years until today each criminal is responsible not only to his immediate neighbours, but to the whole community. We therefore find justice administered in several places, manor court, hundred court, assize court, depending on the nature of the crime and the class of person accused.

Before the Reformation, the power of the Church was immense, in some counties they held nearly half the land. Many felonies were therefore dealt with by the local bishop as lord of the manor, bringing together, in effect, Church and State. Some crimes, if important enough, would be dealt with by the bishop himself as he went round his manors, though normally he functioned through his steward.

In 1348, William White was caught poaching in the bishop's chase at Malvern, and on August 28th in the following year he was summoned to the bishop's palace at Bosbury and had to do homage to the bishop and undertake not to poach again. The bishop was on the round of his manors at the time, and no doubt found it convenient to deal with that case at Bosbury, interviewing William White in private.

The genealogist is naturally interested for it seems curious that so minor an offence should be dealt with at such a high level. Why did the bishop deal with it? Why interview the person privately? What kind of person was William White, and what was the extent of his poaching? Why was he not brought before the Steward at the usual manor court? And why was only William White summoned when there were half a dozen others caught at the same time?

Bishops' registers are in existence for most dioceses, and though they are not always adequately indexed, it is often possible by searching both nominum and locorum to cover the ground. They deal, of course, with the general administration of the diocese, not only with crime and punishment on the bishop's manors. Institutions, for example, greatly help the genealogist by showing the lords of manors generation by generation as they presented, though as regards the incumbent the genealogist takes into account that pluralism was common throughout the Middle Ages. Ordinations, too, record members of the family who passed through the religious or secular degrees.

But we are dealing here more with law than administration, and these registers, though they tell of isolated incidents, such as that mentioned at Bosbury, sometimes disappoint by not giving facts that the genealogist can use. They record the person, and the act, but seen from an angle that is not genealogically useful. Yet, to repeat, when we get back to the period before easily-consulted records, we must pick up facts wherever we can, hoping that the little from several sources will combine to form a picture.

On the practical side, the searcher is advised to visit his local cathedral and inquire whether there is a registry, or cathedral library, where ecclesiastical records are stored. Lambeth Palace, for example, has a library covering most of the see of Canterbury. From there, or from his public library, he will find which of the bishop's registers have been printed. Those of the see of Hereford, for example, have been published by the Cantelupe Society for a period of several hundred years.

On the whole, ecclesiastical manuscripts have not been extensively printed for the cost is prohibitive at the present time. The searcher must often rely on manuscript indexes, if he is lucky enough to find any, and then refer to the originals. If he has no experience of abbreviated latin, he may have difficulty even in deciding if a particular entry is of sufficient interest to be translated. Again, without wishing to be discouraging, archivists are at present so heavily overworked that many months sometimes elapse before one's own work can be done. The private searcher, for that reason if for no other, strives to do all the research he can for himself. And he usually finds, as he works back through the centuries, that he acquires the feel of the years; he begins to anticipate as he reads, knowing from what he has learned before what to expect. Words change, but the form stands : the legal mind does not change fundamentally.

To help him with his initial work *The Handwriting of English Documents* by L. C. Hector can hardly be bettered, dealing with medieval Latin and French, and fully illustrated. But it is a long task, and the beginner is frequently baffled to such an extent that he has no alternative to handing over to the expert.

Fortunately, most of the old cartularies have been published, many in Victorian times, some of them verbatim, so that all the information is there. Unfortunately the indexes are often unsatisfactory, and it may be advisable for the searcher to go through them page by page. If, for example, his family held land of a monastry it is likely that some leases, charters, or records of their tenancy, will be in the cartulary. In early centuries he may even find references to court rolls and wills, though the originals have long since gone. He cannot afford to miss any reference either to his name or to the district where his family lived when he is back in pre-Reformation days.

Sometimes one comes across those astonishing glimpses that carry the searcher back long before the time of proper records. In the Liber Landavensis are copies of grants to the church of Llandaff in the fifth and sixth centuries. Of course, no pedigree can go back so far, no continuity can be established, nor even any certainty that the person was related to the searcher. Yet if the name is uncommon, it is not impossible that the family were living in that area at that time, and it may be possible from the entries to obtain a general idea of their early migrations.

Chapter 13

BILLS AND ANSWERS

M O S T of the records of Chancery are at the Record Office, but as an illustration of the value of documents elsewhere I give an extract from Briefs in Chancery, November to December, 1757, in the manuscript room at the British Museum (Additional MSS). Seldom is the genealogist lucky enough to find such a treature, but when he does a whole section of his pedigree falls into place.

Add. MSS. 36188 f. 236.
Robert Stewart esq plaintiff and Edward Bartlett and
Felix Bartlett defendants 1756

That Thomas Bartlett of Barre co. Staffs esq decd being seised of property in the parish of Castle Moreton and elsewhere in co. Worcs and lands in Staffordshire, Salop, & Montgomery a great many years ago departed this life seised of the same without disposing thereof leaving issue only a son named Rowland and a daughter named Ellen who intermarried with William Stewart esq plaintant's great grandfather.

That the said Rowland Bartlett on the death of his father became seised of the manors and had issue one son Basil Bartlett and no other issue and died seised of the premises without disposing thereof and on his death Basil Bartlett as heir to his father became seised and had issue 4 children, Thomas, William, Frances and Rowland and no other issue and the said Thomas, William and Frances having departed this life without issue Rowland Bartlett the youngest son of the said Basil on his death became seised of the premises as heir.

That the same Rowland Bartlett had issue several sons and daughters (to wit) Henry his eldest son & Frances, Hellen, Catherine, Ann, Thomas, Basil, Winifred, Rowland, Edward, William, Felix and Charles his younger children. That the said

Henry & Thomas died unmarried without issue and Basil the next son on the death of his father became seised of the premises as his heir and the said Frances, Ellen, Catherine, Anne, Winifred, Rowland and Charles died infants and unmarried and the said William departed this life many years since without issue and the said Basil also died seised of the premises in May 1753 without issue leaving Edward and Felix his brothers and no other brother or sister or any of their issue to survive them.

That upon the death of the said Basil Bartlett without issue the said Edward and Felix Bartlett or one of them took possession of the premises and are now in possession of the same notwithstanding the said Edward and Felix Bartlett were educated in the popist Religion or professed the same before they were 18 and so continued to do at the death of Basil Bartlett and ever since and have not taken the oath of allegiance and supremacy nor subscribed the declaration set down in the act in the 30 Car II and by means thereof disabled to take any lands within this kingdom.

That plaintiff is only brother and heir at law of Francis Stewart esq deceased who was the eldest son and heir of Francis Stewart esq plaintiff's late father who was the eldest son and heir at law of Francis Stewart esq plaintiff's grandfather which last mentioned Francis Stewart was the only son and heir of the said William Stewart by the said Ellen Bartlett his wife. There being none of the said family of Bartlett remaining besides the said Edward and Felix who are disabled to take the said premises, plaintiff, as next of kindred who is a protestant, applied to the said Edward and Felix to be let into possession of the said premises which Basil Bartlett died seised of and to have an account of the rents and profits.

Defendants pretended they were entitled to enter the said premises as they had been conveyed to some protestants capable of taking same and in their right defendants receive the rents. That any such conveyance was fraudulent and for no consideration. Defendants contend that the widows of Basil and William who are still living can defeat plaintiff's claim.

F

Defendants contend that the said Ellen Bartlett sister of the said Rowland Bartlett the great grandfather of the said Edward and Felix never intermarried with plaintiff's great grandfather William Stewart or in case she did so intermarry yet that she had no issue by him AND they also pretend that the same Rowland Bartlett had other issue than one son the said Basil Bartlett the grandfather of the defendants and that some descendant from such issue are still living AND also pretend that Thomas Bartlett the eldest son and Frances Bartlett the daughter of the said Basil Bartlett the grandfather were married and left some child or children whose descendants are still living.

Answer of Felix Bartlett defendant

Defendant believes the said Thomas Bartlett left issue an only son named Rowland and three daughters named Amy, Ellen and Mary and that the said Ellen intermarried with one Mr. Stewart of Castle Frome co. Hereford gentleman but whether the said William Stewart was an ancestor of the plaintiffs defendant cannot set forth but leaves the plaintiff to make such proof as he is able. Defendant believes that Rowland, on the decease of his father, became seised of the properties as his heir at law and that the said Rowland had issue 4 sons (sic) viz Basil who died infant Bartholomew and John and two daughters Marey and Ann and that on the death of Rowland his son Basil became seised of the properties as his heir at law. Defendant believes that the said Basil had issue such children as in the Bill and no other issue and that Rowland Bartlett the youngest son of the said Basil, his two elder brothers being dead without issue, became seised on the death of his father as his heir at law.

Defendant believes that the said Rowland had issue such children as in the Bill and the said eldest son Henry died unmarried and that all the other children of the said Rowland are also dead without issue save only defendant himself and his eldest brother Edward Bartlett who is now living and is as well as defendant a bachelor and save Catherine and Winifred Bartlett spinsters two of the defendants' sisters who are now living in Flanders or some other part beyond the seas as defendant believes.

Defendant believes that his late brother Basil Bartlett was at his death and for many years before seised of the following estates—

(Here follow a list of the properties set out in detail with present tenants and terms of tenancies)

That on the death of Basil the said Edward Bartlett as heir at law is possessed of the said estates save those purchased by Mrs Ann Edwards and into which she was put into possession by the said Edward Bartlett on completion of purchase and the estate in jointure to Bridgett Bartlett.

Defendant is a stranger to the pedigree of the plaintiff and therefore cannot set forth whether the plaintiff is heir at law of Francis Stewart and other contentions set out in the Bill and leaves it to the plaintiff to prove his descent.

Defendant admitteth that his brother Basil Bartlett died without issue on 14 may 1753.

That previous to and in consideration of the marriage of defendant's brother William Bartlett (who is dead without issue) with Bridgett Hornyhold & of £800 her portion a jointure was made by defendant's said late brother Basil for her life to take effect on the death of her husband of the estate of Castle Moreton to be in the tenure of Ambrose Lee at £63 p.a. and that a life annuity of £38 was granted by the said Basil Bartlett out of other lands in Castle Moreton as defendant believes as an addition to the jointure of the said Bridgette.

That in consideration of and previous to the marriage of defendant's brother Basil with Mary Arden and £1,300 her portion a term of years was created for raising out of the said estate called Little Dorsington £900 for the use of the said Mary Arden with interest @ 5% p.a. from the decease of the said Basil Bartlett until the money should be raised which said late wives and now widows of William and Basil are now living and claim and enjoy their jointures save that the said Mary Bartlett as defendant believes only receives interest on £900 @ 4%. Defendant, with power granted by his brother,

is desirous of selling the said estates and insists he has a right
so to do.

There is an opinion expressed by T. Phillips dated March
13, 1757 which strongly favours the defendants and suggests
waiting to see if the other defendant puts in his answer.
Robert Stewart, plaintiff, died a very old man on October 6,
1757, shortly after presenting his complaint, and as his
descendants did not have dealings in the properties named by
the defendants, the process may have been discontinued on
his death. The oath of allegiance and supremacy was presumably under one of the Acts passed between 1702 and 1722,
the claim being based on the prohibition of papists to hold
land within the kingdom.

It will be seen that in compiling the pedigree care has been
taken to distinguish between those facts which are agreed by
both sides, and those which are in dispute. Catherine and
Winifred Bartlett, for example, are stated by the plaintiff to
have died infants, whereas Felix Bartlett, in his answer, says
that they are 'now living in Flanders or some part beyond the
seas'. All the genealogist can do in the absence of other information is to note both statements and wait until he can
verify one or the other.

Similarly with the children of the first Thomas Bartlett,
Amy and Mary, and those of the first Rowland Barrett
(Bartholomew, John, Mary, and Ann). These may be actual
issue, or inserted by the defendant to confuse the plaintiff.
They can only be put into the pedigree tentatively until the
registers, or some other source, can confirm their births.

There is a difference between Henry and Thomas Bartlett
who are both known to have died unmarried, and Frances,
Ellen, Anne, Rowland, and Charles who died infants. From
the point of view of issue, it may be the same, but the facts,
such as we know them, are as shown, and that is what we
show. The information about the wives of William Bartlett
and Basil Bartlett are taken from the details of the land which
I have omitted from the above extracts.

STEWART *v.* BARTLETT
(Names in brackets are those disputed)

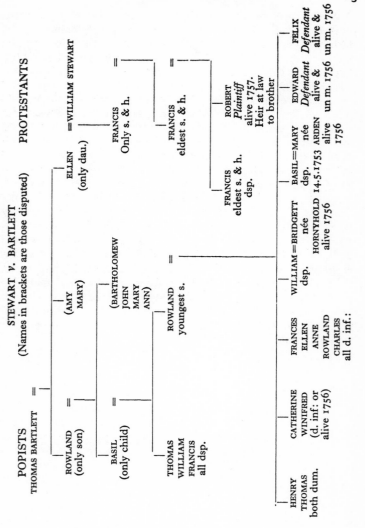

POPISTS

THOMAS BARTLETT =

PROTESTANTS

ELLEN
(only dau.)
=WILLIAM STEWART

ROWLAND
(only son) =

(AMY
MARY)

FRANCIS
Only s. & h.

BASIL
(only child) =

(BARTHOLOMEW
JOHN
MARY
ANN)

ROWLAND
youngest s.

FRANCIS
eldest s. & h.

THOMAS
WILLIAM
FRANCIS
all dsp.

=

FRANCIS
eldest s. & h.
dsp.

FRANCIS
eldest s. & h.

ROBERT
Plaintiff
alive 1757.
Heir at law
to brother

HENRY
THOMAS
both dum.

CATHERINE
WINIFRED
(d. inf: or
alive 1756)

FRANCES
ELLEN
ANNE
ROWLAND
CHARLES
all d. inf.:

WILLIAM=BRIDGETT
dsp.   née
HORNYHOLD
alive 1756

BASIL=MARY
dsp.   née
14.5.1753 ARDEN
alive
1756

EDWARD
Defendant
alive &
un m. 1756

FELIX
Defendant
alive &
un m. 1756

A discovery of this kind, in the absence of other information, opens up many avenues of search—for example, in the Record Office are documents relating to recusants which might contain entries of Bartletts. Four generations are covered by this one document, and mention of land in four counties. There are probably Inquisitions Post Mortem, and two likely sources are the wills of the widows of William and Basil Bartlett, both of whom were alive in 1756, both without issue. Also the wills of Edward and Felix Bartlett, both alive and unmarried in 1756. What age were they then? Did they ever marry? If not, to whom did the property descend, for it looks as if the whole branch died out? Of course, the fact of Robert Stewart being nearly ninety, at the date of the Bill does not mean that Bartletts of the same generation were also old. Yet they do not appear to have been very young, for they were the surviving members of a large family, and at least two of them were married. But we dare not enter on the pedigree that Edward and Felix dum., all we know for certain is that they were unmarried at the date of the Bill. They could, to take an imaginary case, be children of a second marriage of Rowland Bartlett, born long after the rest of the family, attacked by an old and distant cousin, Robert Stewart. One can imagine many situations in which the pedigree, as it stands, would fit.

Chapter 14

CHANCERY PROCEEDINGS

R E C O R D S of the Chancery cover many thousands of manuscripts from earliest times to the nineteenth century. Some of these we have already considered—Charter Rolls, Inquisitions —later we shall consider Fine, Close and Patent Rolls, some of the great sources of information for the genealogist as well as the historian.

Chancery Proceedings vary in their usefulness, sometimes of little use, at other times, as mentioned in the last chapter, giving the genealogist information which if gathered from other sources would take him far longer.

Calendars and indexes are available, often in local libraries, though the original manuscripts are now at the Record Office in London. If the searcher has a choice, if there are for example many entries under his name and he has to select which to have examined, he should choose those where plaintiff and defendant have the same name. They are more likely to be family disputes, whereas some, if not most, of the others will be no more than commercial suits such as the recovery of debts. Even those, of course, are useful for they will fill in some of the background, where a member of the family traded, perhaps giving his trade for the first time.

C.1/28/455-469 2 Edw. IV (1461/3)

Complaint by Francis de Jwngent of Barcelona, patron of the galley 'St. Anthony & St. Francis' of Barcelona, against Nicholas Carmynow, Thomas Tregarthyn and many others, owners of the barge 'Marcell' of Fowey and ship 'Edward' of Polruan re seizure of galley with goods to the value of £12,000 at Plymouth, in spite of letters of safeguard from the late King Henry—

This particular suit covers fifteen membranes, with many

answers and lists, and only relates to the seizure of goods, unlikely to be fruitful for the genealogist unless he is particularly interested in this transaction. It is more likely that the names are all he can use.

But more human problems often emerge, where, though the facts for the pedigree are few, the background is richer.

C.1/5/40 6 Hen IV—2 Hen VI (1404-26)

Complaint made to the Bishop of Durham, Chancellor of England, by Hamon Coppe of Elmstede, co. Kent, cordwainer against William Evot of Bircheholt, co. Kent gentleman that the latter on the feast of the Circumcision 4 Hen V with others came to his house in Elmstede and to William Fuller being there and threatened his life and limbs and took him and imprisoned him to his great damage and loss of his goods while William Fuller found two pledges, to wit Henry atte Wode and Esmond Pynnok who were bound to Evot in £10 to have William Fuller at the Court of Dover to answer Evot. Notwithstanding Fuller was there Evot sent for Esmond and showed him a scroll and said the same was a warrant to take him to Canterbury Castle and keep him there until the day fixed in the warranty if he would not come to agreement with him. Esmond found a pledge and paid him 5 marks, but by menaces was forced to find a pledge for paying 5 marks at a certain day. Meanwhile the said Evot took out a writ of debt in the Common Bench against Henry atte Wode, the other pledge on the same obligation. He begs Evot may be examined and forced to make restitution to Esmond and to Henry his costs and damages and the bond cancelled. On the feast of Epiphany 4 Hen V he went to plaintiff's house and made assault and battery and took him and imprisoned him in Dover Castle until he had paid £10 for his deliverance and he still menaces and threatens him in life and limb. He desires Evot may be punished for these extortions and that plaintiff may go tranquilly about his business.

This shows that the defendant was in Elmstede on the feast of the Circumcision 4 Hen. V Establishing a person's whereabouts is one of the hardest tasks of the genealogist, for a man is often described as 'of a particular place' simply because he owned property there. When another property is dealt with he will be described as of that, the same man having apparently many names, yet identified from the point of view of residence with none. A Chancery Proceeding may not prove that he lived permanently in a specified neighbourhood, but it does show that he was there on a certain date. If he is found there in other documents spread over perhaps several years, one might assume that he lived at all events part of his life in that district. When, therefore, one finds the same name in another part of the country it probably indicates another member of the family. Thus the genealogist circumscribes his characters, discovering little incidents that place them, not only topographically, but socially, and perhaps commercially. Here, for example, the plaintiff is a cordwainer, and the defendant a gentleman.

In another suit, some thirty years later, we find a man of the same name 'a trewe liegeman of our sovereyn lord the Kyng' as of Byrcholte, Kent. There is nothing to indicate the age of the person in either suit, so we cannot tell if it is the same, but the indications are that if not the same, they are of the same family—

C.1/20/16 32-3 Hen VI (1453-55)
Complaint made to the Archbishop of York, Chancellor of England, by William Evot of Byrcholte, Kent 'a trewe liegeman of our sovereyn lord the Kyng' that whereas complainant made William Scot 'your uncle', now Sheriff of Kent, to be jointly enfeoffed with complainant in certain lands and tenements in Braybourne and Wye co. Kent, to the value of £40 and William Scot desired to hold to farm a parcel of the same land paying yearly to complainant 20s., but seeing the law would not compel him to pay, the said William Scot has held the same for 20 winters and more without payment amounting to over £20. Complainant held lands of the said Scot in Bircholt in fee farm at 40s. a year and Scot, taking advantage of his office of Sheriff has entered into the same and ousted complainant and on Whit Sunday last caused him to be

arrested in his parish church and cast into a cart and took him
to Canterbury Castle and put him and his two sons in prison
among felons till 'they were fain to be bound in a great sum
to stand at his own ordinance'. He herewith seeks redress.

From this the genealogist sees that the complainant was
enfeoffed in lands in Braybourne and Wye co. Kent, to the
value of £40, and that a parcel of that land was worth yearly
twenty shillings. This leads him back to Inquisitions Post
Mortem and ad Quod Damnum from which he may be able to
trace the land through succeeding generations.

When we come to suits between members of the same
family we often find not only the genealogy set out, as in the
suit between papists and protestants, but the land described
about which the suit is held. This provides an approach from
two directions.

C.3 Series 2. U.183/25 (1558-79)

Complaint made by John Underwood that Roger Underwood
his grandfather was lawfully seised by ancient course of inheritance in a messuage and 40 acres of land meadow &
pasture in Barlaston co. Staffs & so seised he conveyed the
same to his son John father of the complainant & Alice his
wife complainant's mother & their issue. John & Alice entered
into the same and had issue the complainant. About a year
ago John & Alice being aged & impotent & for other con-
siderations conveyed all their right & title in the same to
complainant and his issue, by force whereof he is now solely
seised of the same and takes the issues and profits thereof.
The deeds concerning the said conveyance to John & Alice &
divers other deeds concerning the same have come into the
possession of Humfrey Underwood & William Snape, who by
force thereof have entered into the premises and taken the
profits and have conveyed to themselves & to others to their
use divers estates therein & he desires they may be called to
appear to answer the same.

Answer of Humfrey Underwood & William Snape

That the premises in question being a messuage or dwelling
house & a yard & 8 acres of land in Barleston were lawfully

seised in his lifetime by John Underwood grandfather of the said Humfrey & about 90 years ago he died thereof seised & the same descended to his son and heir John Underwood the younger & he died seised thereof about 22 years ago whereupon the same descended to his son and heir the said Humfrey who entered into the same and is lawfully seised thereof & the said Roger & John complainants grandfather & father by their deed ready to be shown to this court ratified & confirmed the said Humfrey's title therein & bound themselves to grant the same to Humfrey & his heirs for ever. So being seised, Humfrey, after the said confirmation demised a moitie of the premises to the said John Underwood father of the complainant for a term of certain years yet enduring at a certain yearly rent & the other moitie he demised to Margaret now wife to the said William Snape & the said John Underwood, father of the complainant & the said William Snape entered into the same. They deny the premises descended as stated in the complaint.

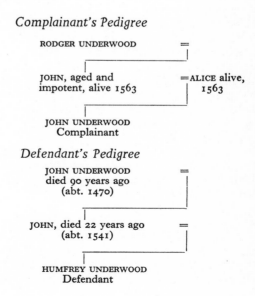

Complainant's Pedigree

RODGER UNDERWOOD =

JOHN, aged and impotent, alive 1563 =ALICE alive, 1563

JOHN UNDERWOOD
Complainant

Defendant's Pedigree

JOHN UNDERWOOD
died 90 years ago
(abt. 1470) =

JOHN, died 22 years ago
(abt. 1541) =

HUMFREY UNDERWOOD
Defendant

Here, in a particularly difficult period for the genealogist, we have considerable information about a family who appear to be of the prosperous yeoman class. Poor people, as we have seen, had their disputes settled in the manor courts; here we have the type of complaint and answer that form a large part of Chancery Proceedings.

Occasionally we come across depositions of witnesses giving us glimpses into the life of a particular person, like a searchlight illuminating a small object while all round is darkness. At the end of a suit over the disposal of property held by creditors are the following, sworn on October 28, 1788, at 'the house of James Morgan known by the sign of the crown in Stone'—

Mary Beardmore of Heath House Checkley spinster aged 39 has known complainant John Phillips & all defendants except Grepton & his wife for 7 years but does not know other complainants. Also knew Thomas Cotton late of Cotwalton who died about 1 year ago.

Hugh Wheatley of Stone gent aged 30 knows all complainants & defendants & for 3 years knew Thomas Cotton deceased by whom he was employed as his attorney & that he died nearly 2 years ago.

William Ratcliffe of Cotwalton farmer aged 64 known all complainants & defendants except complainants William Emery & John Phillips & defendant Sarah Grepton. Will of William Cotton produced who died 13 or 14 February 1773 & was buried at Stone.

William Harding of Cotwalton farmer aged about 50 has known Thomas Underwood for 20 years or upwards.

John Swinnerton of Sugnall gent aged 54 knew Thomas Underwood for several years.

This is one of the few places where ages are given, thus enabling the genealogist to reach at least an approximate year of birth. So often in his searches he would like to know the age of people. Lack of that information leaves doubt about which generation a certain person may belong to. Where sons took the Christian names of their fathers, confusion between generations is unavoidable.

Chapter 15

FINE ROLLS AND PATENT ROLLS

N o w we come to what must be one of the most wonderful series of documents of any country in the world—Fine Rolls, Patent Rolls, and Close Rolls, of which the first two will be dealt with in this chapter.

It is not easy to define the precise matters covered by each series for they overlapped, and if a searcher was presented with an entry he might find it difficult to know from which source it came. There are, however, broad divisions. Fine Rolls record fines levied on behalf of the king for permission to perform certain acts, such as to alienate land, or for heirs to come into their inheritance, for letters of protection for those travelling abroad, for grants of wardships and marriages. A large part of the king's income came from these fines. They are the old equivalents of our modern taxes for keeping dogs, having television, driving cars, using guns. Fine Rolls (originally Oblata Rolls) run in an almost unbroken sequence from 1 John to 1641, over five hundred rolls.

In addition to the fines, however, we have the writs *de diem clausit extremum* which set up the Inquisitions Post Mortem; also patents for the appointment of sheriffs and escheators. The following entries show the kind of information they provide—

16 June 1290 Pardon for a fine of £10 to Walter le Venur of all trespass of vert & venison during the time when he was keeper of the forest of Feckenham in that forest until Trinity 18 Edw. I.

17 April 1290 Order taking into the King's hand the manors of Tunnebrigg, Ealdingg and others in co. Kent and others elsewhere (named), Gilbert de Clare, earl of Gloucester and Hert-

ford having rendered into the king's hands all his lands in the realm.

6 July 1332 Order to Robert Selyman, escheator . . pursuant to an Inquisition made by William Trussel . . showing that John de Poultesholte held in chief certain lands in Chitumersh . . and the manor of Poutesholt of John de Wylyton by knight service . . and that John Enok of Poterne, son of William Enok, his kinsman, is his next heir and of the age of eighteen years . . to deliver to John Enok the said lands held in chief, he having done fealty, and to meddle no further . .

Here we have genealogical information both of the land held, and the nature of tenure. We do not know what kind of Inquisition was taken by William Trussel, but it looks like one on the death of John de Poultesholte, and a search of the Inquisitions Post Mortem would probably reveal it.

28 March 1382 Commitment to William Daune, clerk, harbinger of the King's household . . by mainprise of William Evot & William Baybrok, citizens of London . . of the keeping of a built messuage, 37 acres of arable land, 50 acres of pasture, 5 acres of meadow and 20 acres of wood in the parishes of Lamberhurst, Brenchesley & Hadelho, late of John Covesherst, traiter, of the county of Kent, deceased, who was convicted for divers felonies and treasons, to hold, etc., rendering 26/8d. yearly at the Exchequer.

With such precise details of the property, lying in three parishes, it should not be difficult to identify it, and, if necessary, to trace its ownership. These documents are like posts in a wasteland, one goes from them in many directions, sometimes having to return to them before setting off in another direction. If one was interested, for instance, in the family of Covesherst one would have from this entry some at least of his property, and a base from which to make further searches.

Sometimes, too, references are made to the Patent, or Close Rolls, a study of all three sources often enabling one to complete from one source what is missing in another.

Entries appointing sheriffs and escheators may not be useful to many, but there are also the appointments of tax collectors, presumably working under the escheator. Even the bare record that a member of the searcher's family was so appointed establishes the status of the family at that time.

It should be remembered, however, that members of a family did not all have the same status. The head of a family might be an esquire, his eldest son a gentleman, but other sons, kept out of the inheritance of the main land, might be yeomen. The fact of someone being appointed to collect a tax gives that person some status, lifts him above the great yeoman class; but it is only a small addition to the searcher's information.

Patent Rolls cover the period 3 John to 64 Victoria, being enrolments of Letters Patent written on open parchment over the Great Seal. As they were not private, they were left open (hence 'Patent') whereas Close Rolls were sealed and addressed to private persons, or at least dealing with personal matters.

Like Fine Rolls, they deal with the enfeoffment of land, the admission of tenants, the granting of privileges, but in cases where the public was interested. They border also on Charter Rolls, where the crown granted markets, and fairs, the differences being mainly in the form of document, witnessed, or not witnessed. The searcher cannot afford to miss any of these series for he cannot be sure in which one he will find his information.

Most genealogists search these sources in a general rather than a specific way. They start by searching the indexes under the family name and the name of the district in which they lived. This inevitably means that the searcher returns to them as his pedigree grows and as new names and districts come to light.

12 May 1308 Licence, upon fine, for Robert de Bramlyng to grant the manor of West Bramlyng, co. Kent, together with the advowson of the church of that place, held in chief, to Stephen le Cunvers & Matilda his wife and her heirs, & for them to regrant the same to him for life.

Here we have a simple grant to a man and wife with reversion to their children, the manor being regranted to the original grantor for life. There were many manoeuvres of property to ensure that it did not fall into the king's hands. Infant mortality was high, and only a few of the issue of a marriage normally survived. From this grant it might be guessed, but it is only a guess, that Matilda was the daughter of Robert de Bramlyng. Before entering such a relationship in the pedigree, the genealogist would require proof, and the first place to search would be the Inquisitions Post Mortem to see if there was one for Robert de Bramlyng after 1308. If there was nothing in the index, a search would be made for the manor. Failing that, the operation of the advowson would be traced through the bishop's registers to see who appointed to the living in the early fourteenth century.

Next we have a typical Patent Roll entry, concerning a matter of general interest, a document that Bartholomew atte Wode might have produced if his authority had ever been challenged—

14 June 1362 Appointment of Bartholomew atte Wode to take hewers of stone, called 'hardehewers' and other workmen and labourers to dig and cut the stone which the King has caused to be purveyed in Maydenstane quarry for the works in Westminster Palace and put them to work in the quarry to stay there, at the King's wages as long as shall be required; also to arrest all such as he finds contrariant or rebellious and imprison them until he gives orders touching their punishment.

We are inside the working of the State. The authority gives a new interest to the material world, the buildings are more than stone; they are sweat, and tears. We would like to see that quarry at Maidstone—also Bartholomew atte Wode.

Next, another common entry, concerned with the alienation in mortmain, always troublesome in medieval times for it restricted, indeed ended, subsequent fines—

30 November 1365 Licence for the alienation in mortmain by

John Fletcher (and others named) to the Abbot and convent of Boxele, in satisfaction of £7 of £10 yearly of land and rent which they have the King's licence to acquire, of 4 messuages, 89½ acres of land, 8 acres of meadow, 93 acres of pasture, 11½ acres of wood, 14 acres of marsh, 26/10d. of rent and a rent of 1 qr. of palm barley (ordei palm), a hen, half a hen and 3 eggs, in Boxele (Boxley), Eylesford (Aylesford), Stapleherst, Hoo in the parish of Hoo St. Werburg, and Maydestane (Maidstone), not held in chief, which messuages, lands and rent of barley etc., are of the value of 76/6¼d. yearly, beyond a rent resolute, as has been found by inquisition taken by John de Tye, escheator in the county of Kent.

The Statute of Mortmain was rendered inoperative by the method of transferring title by fictitious law suits. For that reason, the genealogist is careful how he interprets fines and licences.

Lastly, an example from the late fifteenth century to show that these rolls are full of interest for the historian—

31 May 1482 Whereas by an Inquisition taken at Dysse co. Norfolk . . . it was found that John Burbage . . . of Bishop's Lenn and Master Nicholas Emnyth of the same, clerk, on 20 October 19 Edw. IV at Lenn aforesaid in the street called 'le cheker' within a messuage late of Walter Cony and before that of John Gavuse . . . under a sill (cardine) of a chapel within the messuage, commonly called 'a threshold', broke ground and dug to a depth of 3 feet and there found and carried off hidden treasure, 1500 pieces of coined gold called 'oldnobles' in two bags of leather; the King hereby pardons to the said John Burbage and Nicholas the said pieces of gold.

There are untold treasures in these bulky volumes, and the genealogist will find them endlessly rewarding, just reading through them even when they do not immediately concern him or his pedigree.

Chapter 16

CLOSE ROLLS

As explained, these were documents of a private nature, sealed up, sent to the individual concerned, or to the escheator or other government representative in the county. This enormous series comprises more than twenty thousand rolls from John to the twentieth century (1903), covering so many subjects that it is impossible to classify them. As with the other great series of rolls, the genealogist will probably go through them during his initial search, returning as other fields open and new names and places are added to his list.

One of their greatest values is the minute picture they give of life through the centuries. When the genealogist reaches the stage of placing his facts in a setting, these Rolls give a better picture of the state of his part of England than can any history. This is most valuable when he is back in the early centuries, for national events often had little impact on the family tucked away on its manor. Instead of the historian setting his family against the background of the French wars, or the suppression of the Welsh, he sets them in the events of their county, or, better, of their local town. In the Close Rolls he will find these small events, overlooked by national historians, but giving him the exact climate of the times in which his family lived. As an example, a member of one family in which I was interested died at Ledbury a few days after the battle there between Prince Rupert and the Commonwealth forces in the Civil War. That event is only mentioned in the most detailed histories, for it was little more than a skirmish. Yet to someone living in Ledbury at the time it was more important than all the French wars, the Reformation—even the Norman Conquest. Men were fighting in the main street, perhaps outside the windows of the room in which this man lay dying. That, for the family historian, is the history that matters. Admittedly, it, in turn, needs to be placed in the wider setting, but these little facts, disturbances, battles, rapes, and murders, appear in the Close Rolls and show the man's little world throbbing round him.

I will not trouble the reader with examples, because unimportant matters are only of interest when they concern the family, or the place, on which he is working. Here is just one—

8 July 1322 To Robert de Hungerford, keeper of certain lands of certain rebels in co. Wilts. Order to restore to John de Poltesholte his lands, goods & chattels . . .with the issues thereof . . . which were taken into the King's hand . . . because John wore at one time the robes of John de Wylinton, knight, a late rebel . . . that John de Poltesholte at no time adhered to the rebels by consent, procuration or councel . . .

Instead, I will follow up the Inquisition Post Mortem referred to in Chapter 7 and show how the Close Rolls expand and fill in details missing from other sources. The reader will remember the I.P.M. on John Evot. The same subject is here seen from a different angle, in fact it deals with a different property, thereby indirectly confirming from another source the facts given in the Inquisition—

Westminster 4 Nov. 1436 To John Mitchell mayor of the city of London & Escheator. Order to remove the King's hand and meddle no further with a tenement and quay adjacent in Brecaxlane in the parish of Allhallows upon the Solar in Thamystrete London delivering to Thomas son of Bartholomew atte Wode any issues thereof taken; as it is found by inquisition taken before Henry Frowyke late mayor and escheator that John Evot at his death held no lands in the mayor's bailiwick in fee simple of the King nor of others but that Thomas Lincoln, Robert Luton draper and Richard Osbarne citizens of London were seised of the said tenement & quay, which is held of the King in free burgage, & by charter indented made a demise thereof to Thomas son of

William Evot citizen and draper of London & to the heirs of
his body, remainder to William son of the said William, remainder to the said John, being the bastard son of William
Evot the father, and to the heirs of his body, remainder to
William son of John Holden of the parish of Hunton co. Kent,
remainder to Lawrence, Thomas & Roger sons of the said
Bartholomew, by name a tenement & quay in the said lane &
parish sometime of Simon de Wynchecombe citizen and
armourer of London between tenements sometime of Gregory
de Rokesle on the east & of Henry Darcy on the west, the
High Street on the north and the river Thames on the south,
which the grantors & William Evot late draper of London had
by enfeoffment of John Seymour, John Clee draper, William
Herston, Matthew Rede & Richard Persoun citizens of London,
that Thomas son of William Evot & William the son are dead
without issue, that after their death John Evot was thereof
seised in fee tail, and died seised of that estate and none other,
that William son of John Holden died without issue before the
death of John Evot, that Lawrence son of the said Bartholomew
likewise died in his lifetime without issue, that Thomas son of
Bartholomew is yet living and of the age of 50 years & more,
that Roger the third son likewise died in the lifetime of John
Evot, & had issue a son John of the age of 24 years & more,
& that John Evot has no heir for that he was a bastard.

To the escheator in Kent. Order to take the fealty of Thomas
son of Bartholomew atte Wode & to give him livery of a third
part of the manor of Westbramlynge otherwise Pympe, and
the issues taken thereof; as it is found by inquisition, taken
before the escheator, that John Evot at his death held no lands
in Kent in fee simple of the King or of others, but that John
Clee, Richard Amory, Robert Luton & Richard Orgare were
seised of that third part, & with licence of the King made a
demise thereof to Thomas son of William Evot, remainder to
Robert son of the said William, remainder to William son of
the said William, remainder to Margaret daughter of William
the father, remainder to Alice daughter of the said William,
remainder to Margaret late the wife of William the father for
her life, remainder to John Evot etc., with the remainders over

(as in the last), that Thomas, Robert, William, Margaret & Alice, sons and daughters of William the father are dead without issue, & Margaret his wife is dead, and that after their death John Evot was seised of the said third part in fee tail, and died seised of that estate and none other, that William son of John Holden died in his lifetime without issue, that Lawrence & Roger sons of the said Bartholomew died in the lifetime of John Evot, & and the said Thomas his son is still living, and that the said third part is held in chief by the service of the third part of one knight's fee; & the king has taken the homage of the said Thomas.

To the pedigree built up from the Inquisition Post Mortem is added in brackets the additional information from the Close Rolls.

As usual, the searcher is led into other subjects: he wants to know more about this tenement and quay in Brecaxlane, and about Allhallows upon the Solar. In the *Dictionary of London* he finds the following—

Allhallows upon the Solar—All Hallows called 'super solarium' 1454—All Hallows the Less upon the Cellar 1322? All Hallows the Less lies on the south side of Thames Street. The church is spoken of as standing on vaults, hence the name, & early deeds (1306 and 1347) speak of tenements under the church.

Brecaxlane—Bretask Lane in Dowgate Ward, leading down to the Thames. Some time prior to 1343 this lane had been closed up by Thomas de Porkeslee, who owned the house in the lane, called la Bretaske and the warf adjoining it, for in 1343 an inquest was held by the Mayor and Aldermen & men of Dowgate Ward as to this obstruction, and the lane was declared 'communis omnibus hominibus'. In 3 Henry VIII the Dyers Company claimed this lane, but the claim was disallowed, and the lane was found to be a common lane of the City and not the Company's. Name derived from the house la Bretask standing in the lane.

THE FAMILY OF EVOT

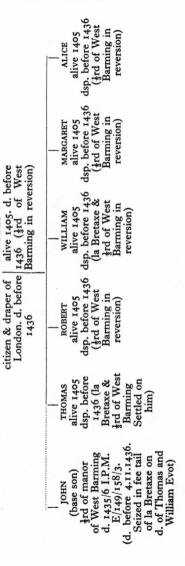

WILLIAM EVOT = MARGARET
citizen & draper of | alive 1405. d. before
London. d. before | 1436 (⅓rd of West
1436 | Barming in reversion)

JOHN
(base son)
⅓rd of manor
of West Barming
d. 1435/6 I.P.M.
E/149/158/3.
(d. before 4.11.1436.
Seized in fee tail
of la Bretaxe on
d. of Thomas and
William Evot)

THOMAS
alive 1405
dsp. before
1436 (la
Bretaxe &
⅓rd of West
Barming
Settled on
him)

ROBERT
alive 1405
dsp. before 1436
(⅓rd of West
Barming in
reversion)

WILLIAM
alive 1405
dsp. before 1436
(la Bretaxe &
⅓rd of West
Barming in
reversion)

MARGARET
alive 1405
dsp. before 1436
(⅓rd of West
Barming in
reversion)

ALICE
alive 1405
dsp. before 1436
(⅓rd of West
Barming in
reversion)

THE FAMILIES OF HOLDEN AND ATTE WODE

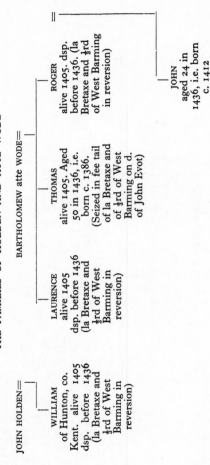

JOHN HOLDEN=

    =BARTHOLOMEW atte WODE=

WILLIAM
of Hunton, co. Kent. alive 1405 dsp. before 1436 (la Bretaxe and ⅓rd of West Barming in reversion)

LAURENCE
alive 1405 dsp. before 1436 (la Bretaxe and ⅓rd of West Barming in reversion)

THOMAS
alive 1405. Aged 50 in 1436, i.e. born c. 1386. (Seized in fee tail of la Bretaxe and ⅓rd of West Barming on d. of John Evot)

ROGER
alive 1405. dsp. before 1436. (la Bretaxe and ⅓rd of West Barming in reversion)

JOHN
aged 24 in 1436, i.e. born c. 1412

La Bretas in the parish of All Hallows the Less. In 1334 Nicholas de Farndon gave it under the name of le Bretasse in Thames Street to Thomas de Porkele (Hustings I. 397) from whom it had passed by purchase prior to 1343 into the possession of Richard de Basynstoke, with the wharf adjoining, (Hustings I. 567). In a view requested by Richard de Basynstoke in 18 Edw. III it is described as supported on eight posts driven into the soil of the City. (Letter Bks. City of London F.p. 97) The name of the house probably implies it was fortified.

It is unlikely that he will be satisfied even with this, for he is now back in fourteenth century London and will want to turn to the original sources of that information (Letter Books of the City of London, and the Hustings Court records). Thus he is led on and on, and sometimes away.

In the reign of Henry VIII a subdivision was made of State Papers, Domestic and Foreign, and the searcher, when he has examined the Close, Fine and Patent Rolls should turn to them for they contain many entries that formerly were in those series. The designation State Papers suggests that they are concerned exclusively with such matters as correspondence and agreements between states, and government matters of no interest to private individuals. Many are, it is true, of this nature, but a mass of ordinary documents, including for the reign of Henry VIII the Patent Rolls themselves, are in this series, and the genealogist cannot afford to miss them during his general search.

Documents coming under the general heading of State Papers are also of great value to students of the Commonwealth period, for they supplement other sources which are often incomplete. At Lichfield, for example, Commonwealth forces not only stole the cathedral plate, and in October 1651 ripped the lead off the roof, but stole and burned masses of records in the custody of Mr. Noble, the Town Clerk.

Similarly, when Wat Tyler's mob was on the march, one of their functions was the destruction of title deeds, and of documents giving authority to those who held mastery over them (such as that to Bartholomew atte Wode).

Some gaps in our records are, it is true, due to expropriation by holders of important offices, such as the kings' secretaries, and this accounts for the Cotton, Harleian, Lansdown and other collections now in public ownership, gathered together by collectors and presented to the nation. So, when gaps are found, they can sometimes be made good from these other sources. University Libraries for example, or the British Museum.

Chapter 17

PIPE ROLLS, PLEA ROLLS, CURIA REGIS, DE BANCO, AND FINAL CONCORDS

STATING that the Fine, Patent and Close Rolls form the greatest series of documents available to the genealogist should not imply that the other series, Pipe and Plea Rolls for example, can be dismissed as unimportant. Distinguished families who have taken part in national events will be found in documents of national importance, and suggestions for these searches will be made later, but even great families have junior branches, and even if one member of a family was distinguished there will be many others, indeed the majority, who will be traced through the sources we have been considering.

The Pipe Rolls are the earliest records after Domesday, covering the period 31 Henry I to 2 William IV, some seven hundred years, and may in the early years supply the only information the genealogist can find about his family. They are what would today be called the Income and Expenditure Accounts of the counties submitted by sheriffs to the Exchequer. The king's income came from two main sources: from his property scattered throughout the country consisting of rents and the profits from running his manors, and, secondly, what one might call casual income from fines and the many forms of taxation levied by the crown.

We have seen in the Patent and Close Rolls that grants and licences of many kinds were made each usually entailing some payment. The sheriff's task was to collect these payments and to account for them to the Exchequer. On the other hand, the sheriff also acted as banker for the crown, paying out as well as receiving, taking his orders from the Patent, or Close, Letters coming to him. He acted for the king in the area for which he was responsible, accounting yearly by means of a financial statement showing either a sum due by him, if his receipts exceeded his expenditure, or to him if expenditure exceeded receipts. A balance due by the crown was usually carried forward for recovery from the following year's income. Sometimes, in early Norman times, a sheriff was responsible for two counties, but soon, as the activities of the crown grew, some of the work had to be taken over by the escheator, the task of the sheriff becoming increasingly one of administration and discipline.

As the rolls themselves are in abbreviated latin, the searcher may find them difficult to read, and may have to employ an expert. But some counties, Staffordshire for example, have printed their entries, the searcher being able thereby to do his own work.

Generally speaking, the entries refer to tenants in chief, or mesne tenants; it is not usual to find yeomen or husbandmen unless they happened to receive some special grant, or be involved in a penalty such as a breach of frankpledge. The rolls are however useful in tracing the descent of manors during that empty period before the Fine, Patent and Close Rolls begin.

A common practice in early days was for a number of the king's manors, sometimes the majority, to be farmed out to the sheriff on a fixed rent, that is to say, he was liable to pay the fixed rent to the Exchequer and keep any profit himself. In such cases the entries on the Pipe Rolls are few because there was nothing to record apart from the entry accounting for the farm rent. In other cases the sheriff managed the farm, or at least supervised the management, on behalf of the king. We then have instructions coming through about restocking, or repairing buildings, or paying annuities to staff—the many matters that arise in the management of property. The value of this information to the genealogist will be small unless his family lived on one of these manors.

The rolls are, however, of great interest to the historian. In 1175 and 1176, for example, Henry II toured the country holding Forest Courts to try and fine those who had trespassed on the royal domaines, or shown disloyalty during the recent troubles. We see penalties coming through the rolls; the

practical functioning of justice. We also find the work of pre-
paring for these royal journeys. Provisions had to be laid in,
horses provided, for the king travelled with even larger caval-
cades than the bishops. In particular, we see these journeys
reflected in the accounts when the king journeyed against the
Welsh, or Scots. As he moved about the country the sheriff
of each county made the necessary financial arrangements,
and these were all recorded and included in the annual sum-
mary submitted to the Exchequer. But we do tend in this
series to move away from personal records, from the family
happenings on the manor. We are in the realm of national
finance, sheriffs, tenants in chief, property seised for felonies,
or coming into the king's hands on minorities.

When we come to legal proceedings, the records are so
varied and so great that it is impossible to condense them into
a few paragraphs. We have already seen something of their
variety in the Bills and Answers, and Chancery Proceedings.
Plea Rolls is a general term covering such sources as the Curia
Regis Rolls, de Banco and Recovery Rolls, taking us over
almost the whole period from Domesday to our present
century. There is, unfortunately, no central index giving
genealogists references to all the records, he has to go to each
source, find if there is an index, and go through them
methodically.

Justice was administered through several courts, at first by
the king himself as he travelled, then, when that method became too cumbersome, a permanent seat of justice was set up
at Westminster. Soon it was found that justice as administered
in the old manor, hundred, and sheriffs' courts varied so much
that litigants preferred to have their cases tried by more im-
partial judges. Thus the central courts of justice became
larger until they, too, had to be subdivided between civil,
criminal and crown pleas. Thus the genealogist, as he works
back through the centuries, finds his sources gradually con-
tracting, but he also has to remember that small disputes,
those which in fact may concern him most, were until recent
times still decided in the local manor court.

Yet, if his records go back several centuries, as they will if he has searched Close, Patent and Fine Rolls and covered the ground already suggested on manor rolls, parish registers and wills, it is likely that at some time in his family's history there was a dispute over land. We have seen an example in the dispute between Papists and Protestants, but there are closer disputes between more nearly related members of the family, which are of great value to the genealogist. Whether he finds these in the Coram Rege, or de Banco, or in the Feet of Fines (Feet in the sense of foot, or end, of a Final Concord bringing the action to an end) he can only tell by searching the indexes.

To cover the ground systematically, of course, the searcher must go to the Record Office for nowhere else will he find complete indexes. Some, such as have been printed, may be at his local library, but many are still manuscript indexes compiled by earlier searchers, and these are indispensable if he is to search thoroughly.

Two examples are here given of Final Concords taken from the Historical Collections of Staffordshire—

Westminster 3rd November 1317 *Complainant*: Robert le Blomere and Isabella his wife. *Deforciant or Impedient*: Roger son of Robert le Blomere. *Subject of Fine, and Result*: One messuage, one mill, 6 acres of meadow, 6 acres of wood, 20s. rent and half a carucate of land in Tybynton. Deft. acknowledged the premises to belong to Isabella: And Compts. granted to Defts. the said premises. To hold to Deft. of the Chief Lords of the Fee, etc., for life of Deft. Remainder to John son of John de Wyrleye.

Westminster, on the quindene of Easter 1324. *Complainant*: William de Burmyngham. *Tenant or Deforciant*: Henry de Burmyngham. *Subject of Fine, and Result*: Manor of Burmyngham, the advowson of the church of the same manor, co. Warw., and the manor of Hoggeston and the advowson of the church of the same manor, co. Buck., and one messuage, 3 carucates of land and 6 marks rent in Shutteford, co. Oxon. Henry granted the said tenements to William and his issue male, to hold of Henry and his heirs, for one rose yearly. If William die without issue male, after his decease the said tenements shall revert to Henry and his heirs for ever.

It can be seen from these that whether the suits are genuine, or artificial, they are of great value to the genealogist. They show the family in action, settling its private affairs, ensuring the continuity that all families have tried to attain through the years.

Chapter 18

HEARTH TAXES, MUSTER ROLLS, AND POLL TAXES

JUST as in each family there are certain members around whom the pedigree hangs, so in searches there are landmarks —islands in the sea of records. Throughout our history taxes have been raised, entailing returns to the central taxing authority. Sometimes most detailed returns have been made, and they provide the genealogist with some of his most valuable information. It is as though a searcher in the future were able to turn up all those people living today who paid income tax. From the assessments he could judge the place in society that each member of his family occupied, as well as where they lived, where they worked, and much of their private affairs.

From similar assessments in the past we also learn much, perhaps not as much as one of our present-day tax assessments would show, but, with for example Hearth Taxes, we go right into their homes, just as we did when examining Inventories.

The Hearth Tax was first instituted in 1662, but was abolished in 1689 because it was so unpopular. People objected to showing tax collectors round their houses. It was soon replaced by a window tax, equally unpopular, though it survived into the middle of last century. But lists of Hearth Tax assessments provide the genealogist with inside information about his ancestors, for each town and vill was surveyed, each house inspected. Two shillings was charged on a hearth, and from the lists the genealogist can place each person according to his wealth. As many as ten hearths was not unusual in the largest houses, usually dropping rapidly to four or five for the local gentry, then to the long list of houses with only one. Also of great value are the supplementary lists of those not liable, either because they had no hearths, or because they were too poor to be assessed.

We have thus a complete survey of the country showing each family at home, indicating accurately the style in which they lived. The task of searching the entire country is, of course, too great for most genealogists, but he can take the county in which he knows them to have lived and list each member of his family. He may, of course, if his name is common, find many families in a county without being able to fit them into the pedigree, but from the complete list he should be able to locate each head of a family.

The value of such information for future searches is evident. This tax was levied while parish registers were operating and at a time when wills are particularly rich in information. These three sources alone should enable most genealogists to build up their pedigrees. The searcher, for example, sometimes finds that he cannot account for some member of the family : he knows that he was born at a certain date, but after that loses trace of him : no will, no administration : he does not even know in what parish to search. From Hearth Tax returns, he may find him in an unexpected part of the county and thus open up a new generation. He is unlucky if he finds nothing : no will, administration, or liability to tax, as well as no entry in parish registers. In that case he may have moved out of the county, or perhaps died young with no record of his burial. Records during the Civil War, for example, were badly neglected, some parish registers having an almost complete blank for those years.

Naturally, Hearth Tax returns are not infallible : if a person had two or more houses, he would be taxed on each, and would be shown as the occupant of each (failing a tenant in occupation). But such cases are rare, and the genealogist would soon find in which house he normally resided from the parish registers. For the mass of the people, gentry, yeoman farmers, and free labour, the returns are the first precise information about the householders of England.

Muster Rolls immediately take the searcher into the realm of military records, and their volume is enormous, stretching

H

from Norman times to our own. For more recent records, we have Army, and Navy, Lists, and, if the genealogist is also historian, many regimental histories. When, however, we move back to the sixteenth and seventeenth centuries we find in military records information that adds much to our pedigree. In the Muster Roll of 1539 we have Staffordshire summarized under vills. Here are a few extracts—

Tyttensor—This person is an abull man with a bow and hath as foloith—Thomas Adderley a bowe and a schieff of arrowes. These persons foloing be abull men with billes and have harnes and artillarie as foloith their names—In primis : John Willot a bill Item : Humphrey Venables a gesterne and a sallett. These persons following have harnes and weypons as foloith their names—In primis : John Venables a hors (others named).

The genealogist searches the manor, parish, or borough in which he is interested and finds listed the able-bodied men with the weapons they held. Again, he is led away—this time into a study of arms, for he cannot understand the entries without knowing at least something of ancient weapons. When he knows that a bill is a pike with a long handle to drag men off their horses; a gesterne a short coat of overlapping steel plates, and a salet a steel cap, he begins to see the kind of people with whom he is dealing.

Yet these sources, for the genealogist, provide him with no more than evidence of the existence of a person. There is, it is true, the additional information about his arms, or the number of hearths in his house, but that person is detached from his family, a sole person, to be identified for the pedigree from some other source. The danger here, of course, is that the genealogist, seeing someone of that name in his pedigree may assume that it is the same. But a single name is not con-clusive : it could be father or son. Sometimes one can tell by their age; one might know that the father at that date would be too old to be described as an 'abull man', therefore it must be his son.

The later Muster Roll, 1640, is particularly useful for it

comes near the Hearth Taxes, enabling the genealogist to trace the family, perhaps finding them again if they moved in the interval. The searcher does not ignore an entry because it is in a place where the family, so far as he then knows, did not live. He keeps the information, with all the rest, for the day when it will fall into place. It may indeed turn out to be the one fact needed to bridge a gap.

Lay (as opposed to Clerical) Subsidies, and Poll Taxes, take the searcher back to Norman times and provide him with similar lists of people living in certain places at certain dates, invaluable for the genealogist who wishes to fix the length of time his family were settled in any one place. From lists he can find the approximate date on which his family moved into a certain parish, or hundred, the name not appearing on the earlier list, but appearing on the later. He then turns to other sources, Inquisitions Post Mortem perhaps, or Fine or Close Rolls, to see if he can trace the enfeoffment, or descent.

Few of these rolls have been printed, though a few counties have made extracts of those that concern them. Generally, however, the genealogist must go to the originals, and he may find it best to employ a professional searcher who knows his way about them. He will need, of course, to give the searcher at least the hundred, if not the parish, otherwise he will incur the expense of fruitless searches. If, therefore, he does not know even the county in which his family lived he will do better to try to find that from other sources before going to the Subsidy Rolls. They are for confirmation rather than discoveries.

Subsidy Rolls, which strictly would include the Hearth Taxes, for they were a form of subsidy, as well as Poll Taxes, are among the records of the Exchequer. The subsidy for 1327, for example, was levied on the inhabitants of certain towns who had goods to the value of ten shillings or more. The tax was one twentieth of their movables, the object being to raise money for the defence of the country against the Scots. There was never a shortage of reasons for raising a tax in the old days—any more than there is today.

Chapter 19

KNIGHTS, ESQUIRES, AND GENTLEMEN

WE have so far been dealing with the genealogist whose family was of the yeoman or small gentleman class, the one that most searchers will be concerned with. But sooner or later he will work back to an esquire, or knight, or perhaps to one of the great landowning families. The same records will serve him, he will still have to search Close, Patent, Fine, and Charter Rolls; but other sources will also interest him.

Under the Feudal System, where all land belonged to the king (until the statute of 12 Charles II abolished tenures in capite and by knight service) the knight's land was held by military service, through the tenant in chief. Where the knight held direct of the king, his service would be direct, otherwise he served his immediate lord, the tenant, perhaps a mesne tenant, who stood immediately above him. Below him, the knight had his tenants—esquires and gentlemen—owing him service in money or kind, and they, in turn, their yeomen, copyholders, or husbandmen.

Earlier we saw how land was settled, how enfeoffments made, how the tenant surrendered his land to have it reissued to him and his heirs, thereby retaining it in his family. But service varied, as we have seen, from carting and ploughing to attending the king at his sport. A gentleman did not render the same kind of service as a serf.

The core of tenure was the knight's fee, represented by the holding of land to a certain value, usually 100s., such person being thereby liable to the duties laid down for a knight. This, in Norman times, meant attending the king in war, and many knights were summoned under this system for the Crusades.

But from an early date scutage replaced personal service. There were two reasons: firstly, when a knight's fee was held by an old, or a very young, person service on the battlefield was impossible, therefore a money payment in lieu enabled the lord to hire service: secondly, owing to the system of subinfeudation, knights' fees were often split, portions being held, half a fee by one, half by another, often split into four or more where several heirs inherited. Service in kind could not be rendered in such cases, payment being the only alternative. Scutage therefore became a recognized form of tenure, and where land is thus held the genealogist recognizes it as an honourable form deriving from the knight's fee.

For the genealogist, manor rolls therefore will be of little use; land held by such tenure will not be dealt with in the manor court. On the contrary, manor rolls will record the movement of that same land on the lower level, the knight himself being lord of the manor and probably not appearing on the rolls unless he himself held the courts. The genealogist finds the land passing through the Close Rolls, through Inquisitions Post Mortem, marriage settlements, leases, and charters such as we have already examined.

But among our national archives are special classes of records primarily concerned with knights and levels above. The king, from time to time, partly in the course of raising money, partly to check on his tenants in chief, required returns of the lands they held, divided into knights' fees, with the holders of each fee.

The Libers Niger and Rubeus are the earliest of these, dating back to 1166, followed by the Testa de Nevill, the Book of Aids and Kirby's Quest.

Back in those times, of course, surnames were only beginning, and the genealogist is unlikely to find his family's name in the indexes. He will more probably find the knights taking their names from the fees themselves, his task being to follow the land until it comes into the family name. In practice, he works the other way, back to the time when the name disappears, then back through successive stages by means of the land itself. Unfortunately it does not follow that, say, John de Staynes, lord of the manor of Staynes, was necessarily related to, say, William de Staynes who held the same manor in the following generation, for it may have gone by purchase and not by descent. So while these returns of knights' fees show the holders at certain dates, they prove no blood relationship. For that, Inquisitions Post Mortem are the most valuable, showing not only the type of tenure and the name, but the heir. These returns by tenants in chief supplement that information.

There are, for example, five volumes of Feudal Aids, arranged under counties, built up from Kirby's Quest and the Nomina Villarum containing, as sample entries, the following—

Hereford. 1431 Ricardus Avenell tenet quintam partem un feodum militis in Magna Marcle
Johannes Muchegose et Milo Watter tenent di feodum militis in Castlefrome
Stafford, the Barony of Stafford. 1284/5 Thomas de Titnesovere tenet titnesovere et Le Bech pro i feodum de dicto barone, et baro de rege in capite
1316 Roger de Tytnesore domini villa de Tytnesore

The searcher cannot assume that Roger de Titnesovere, who held the vill of Tytnesore in 1316, is related to Thomas de Titnesovere who held one knight's fee there in 1284/5. They may have been son and father, but there is no evidence to that effect. A genealogist, as a result of these entries, will search other records for a settlement by Thomas de Tytnesore, and in this search he may find it profitable to trace Le Bech as well as Tytnesore as he may through that parcel of land be led to Roger. If, to take an imaginary example, he found that a Roger de Bech held a knight's fee, or part of a fee, in Le Bech in 1316 he might identify both Rogers as the same.

A great deal of this basic research, of course, has already been done, and the genealogist will make one of his earliest searches printed county records. Yet there were many knights' fees: not every one is recorded. County histories, like the landed Gentry and Peerages, have gaps. In any case, a searcher always goes back to the original document, for the information that one genealogist extracts, though it may not be unreliable, will be slanted towards whatever direction his searches require. He will omit facts unimportant to him, but perhaps of great interest to another. Often, indeed usually, the portion of a document of direct interest to a searcher can be summarized in a few lines, the rest he can ignore. Extracts are notoriously unsatisfactory for that reason.

Knighthood, until recently, was not an honour but an obligation, a man being fined for not taking it up. Many men did not wish to be knighted, for it carried with it certain obligations, there are therefore among the records the results of surveys carried out to find which gentlemen had omitted to take up the Order. It was a form of taxation levied for the privilege of contracting-out.

Esquires, on the other hand, were generally heads of armigerous families, the eldest son of an esquire also being an esquire; his younger sons being designated gentlemen. Today, these terms have no meaning, everyone is a gentleman, and most are esquires. But the genealogist, dealing with the past, notes these facts on his pedigree for they place the man precisely on the social ladder. Often such distinctions enable the genealogist to separate members of the family bearing the same Christian names.

Chapter 20

VISITATIONS, AND THE RIGHT TO BEAR ARMS

I N S T E A D of the genealogist working his pedigree back until it merges into some well-known family, he often first becomes interested because he hears of a distinguished family bearing his name and wants to connect himself with it. He finds himself, in other words, with two families, his own which he is working back, and another which he tries to bring down, or expand, until the two fit together.

There are, as we know, some families who have identified themselves with the famous without having proof that they are even of the same stock. Some have gone so far as to assume their arms, and have no difficulty in convincing themselves that they are entitled to them.

One of the outcomes of all this searching may, indeed, be to establish a right to ancient arms.

The three great sources of information about distinguished families are Burke's Peerage, Baronetage & Knightage—Burke's Landed Gentry—Burke's Family Records. Great care is taken to separate fact from fancy, for in some of the early editions, when families were asked to report their ancestors, they started by a statement that one of them came over with the Conqueror. One has to start somewhere, but very few families can prove their pedigrees back so far : the majority of such statements are guesses. A hundred years ago, when most of these pedigrees were compiled, facilities for research were not as good as today, and in the desire to be both old and distinguished some unreasonable assumptions were made.

However, the genealogist can check most of the statements, and as he builds his own pedigree he will automatically prove, or disprove, the facts already recorded. Most of the descents are down to the nineteenth century, so he should have no difficulty in verifying at least the last two hundred years, for he is then among parish registers, wills and local records with which he can easily deal. The difficulty comes when he has worked back to the genuine source of the printed pedigree; not the Conquest, but the point where the record gives dates and identifies members properly. If by that time he has not been able to link his family to the printed record, he has what one might describe as two legs of a body. It is not possible to suggest whether he should concentrate on his own branch, or on the branch already recorded, which may be more distinguished and therefore easier to trace. If, for example, he has an unusual name, and he finds records in, say, the Landed Gentry, of a family of the same name living in a district from which he knows his own family to have come, then he probably assumes, in the absence of facts to the contrary, that both families are the same and will trace the easier branch hoping that he will reach the generation where the fork appears.

But if his name is common, he may by this method do much fruitless work, finding that the family branches away from his own and appears to have some other origin. He can only be guided by the strength of the probability of connection, in many instances restricting himself to his own pedigree even though the search is harder. But he must find that connection, however long it takes, if he is to establish a right to bear their arms.

Arms of some kind, identification by symbols and colours, date back to before history, but heraldry as we know it in this country ripened about the time of the Crusades. It is sometimes said that many coats of arms were illegally adopted by families who had no right to them, and that the College of Arms was founded to stop abuses. Yet it should be remembered that adoption of arms to which one was not entitled was harder in the Middle Ages than today; families were few, everyone knew everyone, one could not easily move to a new district and set up as an armigerous gentleman. There may have been abuses in the sense of illegitimate branches of a family adopting arms without a difference, or the adoption of crests for which there was no authority, but it is doubtful if there was wholesale abuse of the right to bear arms.

If the genealogist finds himself connected to an armigerous family, his next step is to search the Visitation of the county in which they were living. These have been printed under counties, and most libraries have at least the volumes for their own area. These visitations, carried out by Heralds during the sixteenth and seventeenth centuries, were to establish which families were entitled to bear arms so that the registration of their right could be made. Gentlemen were interviewed, and each had to prove that the arms he bore had been borne by at least three generations, and that he was entitled to them by birth. George Skipp of the Upper Hall, Ledbury, in his Note Book for September 21, 1683, wrote—

The Heralds office was kept in Ledbury in their visitation of this county, and they then entered the pedigree & matches & issue of our family for which he demanded 37 shillings fee of my father but was paid nothing.

Many families proved their right for as long as two hundred years, and such pedigrees when entered by the Heralds are of great value to the genealogist. It means that the original grant by the Sovereign was before that date, so the genealogist must either prove his own descent from some member of the family recorded by the Heralds, or work the pedigree back from the earliest date until it joins his own. A family has, of course, no right to assume the arms of another family, even if the name is the same and they live in the same district. Descent must be proved, and the right acknowledged by the College of Arms.

Crests were not common until the middle of the sixteenth century, and if no crest is given in the visitation, its subsequent grant must be found before it can be used. Some families, particularly in Victorian times when the bearing of arms became fashionable, assumed a crest because they thought it more distinguished.

As for the College itself, the genealogist can be assured of the greatest assistance from them. They must charge a fee, for that is how the establishment is maintained. But their experience, and in my knowledge the service they offer, far exceed the fee. They are the authority on arms, and their library contains books and manuscripts unobtainable elsewhere. When the genealogist reaches the stage of working on his arms, he can do no better than refer to them for both further guidance and information.

Mottoes are not part of a coat of arms, no authority is needed for them, and they carry no prestige beyond the fact that a family may have used one for several generations.

Chapter 21

VICTORIA COUNTY HISTORIES, RECORD SOCIETIES, FAMILY AND PARISH HISTORIES

AMONG the thousands of printed books to which the genealogist has access it is hard to choose a few of particular interest for it depends on the kind of information that the genealogist needs. An obscure pamphlet may have pages of gold if it deals with a subject of special interest to him. The splendid library of the Society of Genealogists alone will feed him for a lifetime.

It is also difficult to suggest general lines of inquiry, for the genealogist, even a beginner, will know them. The Victoria County Histories, for example, are some of the best known treasure-houses for the genealogist, enabling him to go into as much detail as he needs. They are the raw material of every family history, no matter how obscure the family, for they go into the land, the holders, tenants in chief, and minor lords. Unfortunately only a few counties have the complete set, but the work continues so far and so fast as funds allow. The cost of each new volume today is enormous, not only printing costs, but the research that goes into an assembly of such facts. Years of work are needed for a single volume.

Of particular interest are the sections on political and social history written on the narrow scene of that single county, emphasising local subjects that would interest local families, giving the genealogist just that picture that is so hard to compose by himself.

In each issue of the Victoria County History are also the Domesday entries relating to that county, usually in full, with present-day towns and vills identified. I have not referred to Domesday before because it is not of great interest to the family genealogist. To the extent that it is a survey of almost the whole country, carried out with minute detail, every acre, manor, and plough, it occupies a unique place in our archives, but is of more interest to the topographer than to the genealogist. It stands in isolation between the Conquest and the great series of records we have been considering. But only those families whose ancestors held land in pre-Conquest days, or acquired it under the Normans, will find records of themselves, and in most pedigrees there is in any case a great gap before the genealogist can establish any continuity. There are families, it is true, who were on their land at the date of the Conquest, and who managed to keep the name intact and associated with the same land, but by the time the genealogist has worked his pedigree back sufficiently far to be able to associate his family with Domesday he will know enough about research to find his own way among the records. In some counties only the first volume of the Victoria County History has been published, and this is sometimes confined to topography, geology, fauna and flora—not very useful for a genealogist—but Domesday is one of the first sources to be transcribed, and usually that, too, is in Volume I.

Then there are the publications of the many Record Societies, some exclusively dealing with parish registers, others with historical documents of all kinds. There are parish register societies in, for example, Lancashire, Shropshire and Staffordshire, while one must not omit the Huguenot Society of London, The Lincoln Record Society, The Record Society of Lancashire and Cheshire, The Somerset Record Society, The Yorkshire Archaeological Society, and many others, details of which the searcher can obtain from his local library.

Perhaps one of the most active and remarkable societies is the Staffordshire Record Society based on the collection of documents in the William Salt Library at Stafford. These volumes have been appearing since 1880 and cover all the major sources of information—Cartularies, Chancery Proceedings, Family Histories, Final Concords, Court Rolls, Fine Rolls, Quarter Session Rolls, Inquisitions, Bishops' Registers, Parish Histories, Plea Rolls, and many other subjects required by historians and genealogists interested in the county.

Before becoming involved in searches of the primary sources, the genealogist should inquire whether the work has already been done and assembled by his local record society. He may be saved an immense amount of work, and, if he was to employ an expert, much expense. It is, however, wise to test the indexes of some of these volumes, sometimes sections are omitted, and if the searcher relies solely on the index he may miss them. An editor, for example, might decide that to print every Hearth Tax entry would so swell the index as to make the cost of printing prohibitive. If, therefore, he finds a volume containing records like that, of Subsidy Rolls perhaps, or juries at Quarter Sessions, he should test the index.

He may also find in such publications short descriptions of a series of records, giving him an understanding of how they came to be kept, for what purpose, and how they fit into the general system of national, or local, records. Sometimes the genealogist finds in an index a reference that seems to refer to a member of his family, but he does not know what the records are. He sees, perhaps, the two volumes of Homberston's Survey, and does not know if they will interest him because he does not know what they are. Local collections have often gathered scattered information for the convenience of the local historian, and he is not only saved time, but brought in touch with sources about which he would not otherwise know.

Family histories, of other people's families, are usually disappointing. There are, however, cases where they can lead to new sources. If, for example, a searcher was dealing with a yeoman family and found a history of the lords of the manor he might learn about the manor rolls, and so be saved time as well as introduced to new sources. The value of these histories vary greatly, depending on the skill and knowledge of the historian. Some contain little more than copies of M.I.'s. in the local church, perhaps with a pedigree carrying the family back to about the seventeenth century. Others, by men who have made genealogy a life work, can lead the searcher on through what may be a dark period in his own family's history. But it has to be remembered that anyone can write a family history, and that if he has enough money he can have it printed. Few family histories are interesting enough, or well enough written, for a publisher to risk his money on it in the normal course of publishing. The genealogist is therefore dealing with a special kind of book, sometimes with no authority behind it.

Parish Histories suffer from the same dangers. Some are written by a local incumbent with little experience of research, collecting a few facts from old books, institutions from Bishops' Registers, copies of some of the tablets on the walls, stencilled and stapled together and laid on the table for visitors to buy. Others are of remarkable skill, from deep research by the author, giving sources and references of great value to later historians. Occasionally one comes across such an astonishing volume as Earl Coningsby's *Collections concerning the Manor of Marden*, a foolscap book of seven hundred pages in which he not only gives copies of court rolls and chancery proceedings, but expresses opinions about the characters of tenants of the manor alive in 1813, when the book was privately printed, and of former times.

The genealogist turns nothing down, the most unpromising source may be the richest; he picks his facts from wherever he finds them, weighing them for accuracy, discarding some, holding others in abeyance, sorting, sifting, only entering on his pedigree what he knows is true.

Of all his sources, the most valuable is the man in the adjacent chair, the stranger fingering his way through some bulky manuscript. I was at the Probate Registry at Birmingham many years ago and began to discuss with my neighbour some trivial matter of the day. He was going through a bundle of administrations that had not at that time been indexed. A few days later he gave me a list of the administrations he had picked out for me.

Local knowledge is better than all the indexes; what a man has gathered into his mind over the years, unrecorded, refined by his own process of discrimination. I have never yet met a disagreeable genealogist: they are the kindest people in the world.

BIBLIOGRAPHY

A s I suggested in the previous chapter, it is difficult to give a list of books for the genealogist as his interests will vary both for period and locality. I have on my shelves, for instance, seventy volumes of *Staffordshire Historical Collections*. These have been of great value to me, but will be of little value to someone whose family is not connected with Staffordshire. I have, similarly, many volumes on Herefordshire, but am not listing them for the same reason.

There are, however, some books of more general use, and I am giving here those that I have bought and used consistently during the years when I was writing a history of my own family—in fourteen volumes—about a million words. They have, in other words, stood up to long and heavy work.

Guide to the Contents of the Public Record Office, HMSO, 1963 2 vols. This not only gives details of what documents exist, but also gives brief but most interesting descriptions of the classes of MSS, and how they came into existence. There is also a list of Regnal years, and a Glossary.

Lewis's Topographical Dictionary of England and Wales, 1848, 6 vols. This is indispensable where a document gives a parish but no county. Every parish is listed, and short histories are given of each county.

National Index of Parish Registers, by D. J. Steel MA, FSG, and others. Society of Genealogists. This is a new series of which, at the time of writing, only two volumes have appeared. Every parish is listed with details of its registers. Vol I deals with sources of information. The whole series will be of great value to genealogists.

Wills and their Whereabouts, 1963, by Anthony J. Camp BA (Hons), Society of Genealogists. This is exactly what it says, and forms the starting-point for work on wills. The information is grouped under counties.

Pedigree Work, 1936, Phillimore & Co, Ltd. This little book (only 7 x 3½in) is one that I have constantly by me as it is full of practical information. It not only has the dates of Saints Days and Fixed Feasts, but a list of Regnal years which I find easier to refer to than that in the Record Office volume.

English Genealogy, by Sir Anthony R. Wagner, Garter King of Arms, 1960, OUP. I suppose one should not say of any book that it is 'the book to end all books on genealogy', but this comes close to it. After simple little books like mine, the genealogist should turn to this for the real voice of authority.

Dictionary of Archaic and Provincial Words, by J. O. Halliwell FRS, 2 vols, 1868. Particularly useful for identifying objects mentioned in inventories though it is not always possible to find a word owing to local names and varieties of spelling.

Record Interpreter, by C. T. Martin BA, FSA, 1892. This is useful for Latin abbreviations, and for a glossary of Latin words that are found in documents. It also gives the Latin equivalent of English names—eg Gulielmus= William.

Dictionary of London, by Henry A. Harben FSA, Herbert Jenkins Ltd, 1918. An invaluable book giving details of old churches, streets, and alleys, and also street plans of London in 16th—18th centuries.

London churches before the Great Fire, by Wilberforce Jenkinson, SPCK, 1917. Perhaps of limited interest to the compiler of a pedigree as it has no genealogical information, but useful for writing the family history.

On more general subjects as opposed to the practical work of building up the pedigree, I have found the following to be helpful with the background of my family history when relating the facts in the various documents to the life of the people of the period. In addition to the series of *The Oxford History of England*, I have—

Growth of the Manor, by Sir Paul Vinogradoff MA, LlD, Allen & Unwin, 1904 (Fifth Impression 1951).

Manor & Manorial Records, by Nathaniel J. Hone, Methuen, 1906. It has many illustrations.

Midland Peasant, by W. G. Hoskins, Macmillan, 1957. Although this is the history of one Leicestershire village, it is typical, and gives a clear picture of the centuries.

Medieval Panorama, by G. G. Coulton, 1949, CUP.

Feudal England, by J. H. Round, Allen & Unwin, 1895 (Reset 1964).

English Society in the Early Middle Ages, by Doris M. Stenton, Penguin, 1951.

When I read the long, comprehensive, and excellent bibliography in *National Index of Parish Registers* (to which I referred earlier) pages 381-439, I realised how limited my own reading has been. I would refer anyone who wishes to go deeply into genealogy and related subjects to consult that list. I have here limited myself to some of the books I have around me. With them, and others that I have not mentioned because of their limited interest, I have managed to write my own family history. One cannot read everything. I could, and perhaps should, have read more, searched more, travelled more, learned more, and so written a better family history. On the other hand, I might never have started it.

INDEX

Persons and places NOT indexed are fictitious